Ancestry.com
Frequently Asked Questions

A Genealogy Reference Source

By Dennis Fitzgerald

Please Leave a Review

Share your thoughts,
let your voice be heard,
In the realm of reviews,
be the shining word.

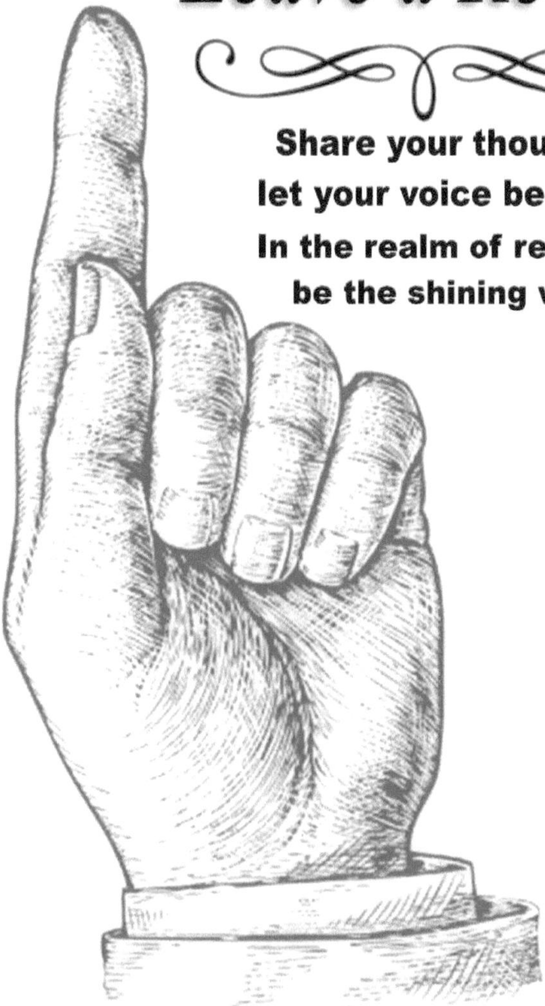

THANK YOU

Introduction

Welcome to Your Guide to Ancestry.com: Frequently Asked Questions" In the pages ahead, you'll find a treasure trove of insights, guidance, and answers to embark on your family history expedition. Whether you're new to genealogy or a seasoned researcher, this book is designed to be your compass, your companion, and your bridge to the past.

Ancestry.com, a platform dedicated to genealogy and historical research, is a dynamic realm that constantly evolves. To navigate it successfully, we've curated a list of common questions that you might encounter. While the website's features may change, these questions serve as timeless signposts, steering you toward the information you seek. As you dive into each chapter and section, remember that your journey of discovery is unique. This book aims to empower you to navigate the Ancestry.com landscape, fostering connections and unlocking stories that resonate through generations.

In this digital age, we've integrated a powerful tool to enhance your experience: QR codes. These compact squares are gateways to a wealth of supplementary information. For those new to QR codes, fear not – using them is simple. If you have a smartphone, follow these steps:

- *Open your smartphone's camera app.*
- *Hold your phone over the QR code.*
- *Let your camera focus, and a notification will pop up.*
- *Tap the notification to access additional content directly on your device.*

Throughout this book, each chapter and major section contains QR codes that link to more in-depth resources on Amcestry.com. These codes are your express ticket to a deeper understanding of the topics covered. From video tutorials to step-by-step guides, they provide an immersive way to explore and learn.

Your journey through "Ancestry.com Frequently Asked Questions " is a testament to your commitment to preserving history and shaping the future. As you embark on this ancestral expedition, remember that every discovery you make contributes to a rich tapestry of stories that will be cherished by generations to come.

Happy exploring! Dennis Fitzgerald

Ancestry.com
Frequently Asked Questions

Chapter 1 32

Introduction to Ancestry.com 32

What is Ancestry and Family History? 32

Question: Can I collaborate with my family members on our family tree? 32

Question: What are some creative ways to preserve my ancestral journey? 32

Question: Any ideas for creative family history-themed crafts or DIY projects? 33

Different Forms of Family History 33

(e.g., books, albums, newsletters) 33

Question: How can I start a family newsletter that engages readers? 33

Question: I'm not tech-savvy, but I want to create a family history book. Where do I begin? 34

Question: How can I incorporate our family's traditions into the project? 34

Question: How can I create a dynamic multimedia presentation for my family? 35

Question: Are there online platforms for creating a digital family archive? 35

Benefits of Creating a Family History 36

Question: What are the benefits of undertaking this family history journey? 36

Question: How can family history positively impact relationships with living family members? 36

Question: What are the emotional benefits of delving into family history? 37

Question: How can knowing my family history improve my overall well-being?..37

Question: Positive influence on children's interest in heritage: 37

When to Start Your Family History Journey 39

Question: How do I start preserving our family's stories? 39

Question: How can I document my family's history digitally without feeling overwhelmed?..39

Question: Concerns about the cost of creating a family history:.............40

Additional Resources:..41

Chapter 2.. 42

Getting Started on Ancestry.com 42

Overview of Available Features and Tools......................... 42

Question: What are the main benefits of using Ancestry.com for ancestry research?...42

Question: Is Ancestry.com suitable for beginners?.................................44

Question: What are the costs associated with using Ancestry.com?.......44

Question: Tell me what tools and features on can help me discover my family history?...45

Question: What are the main features and tools available on Ancestry.com? 46

Question: What are some of the unique features that set Ancestry.com apart? 49

Question: What are the different subscription plans and their benefits?50

Question: What are the pros and cons of using a paid account on Ancestry.com? 51

Question: How can I get started with Ancestry.com? 53

Question: What are the steps to setup a Free account on Ancestry.com 54

Question: What are the steps to setup a Paid account on Ancestry.com 55

I Have Some Concerns Setting up my account. *57*

Question: What information do I need to provide when creating an Ancestry.com account, and how is my data protected? 57

Question: I'm not very tech-savvy. Will I need to download any software to create a Ancestry account? 57

Question: Can I create an Ancestry.com account on my mobile device, or do I have to use a computer? 58

Question: Is it true that Ancestry.com offers its services entirely for free? Are there any hidden costs or subscriptions required? 58

Question: I'm concerned about my family tree's security. Who can view the information I add to my tree on Ancestry? 58

Question: Can I collaborate with other family members on my Ancestry.com family tree? How does that work? 59

Question: I'm worried about making mistakes while building my family tree. Can I undo changes or revert to a previous version? 59

Question: I have physical family documents and photos I'd like to include in my tree. Can I upload them to Ancestry.com? 60

Question: Where can I find resources or tutorials to help me make the most of the platform? 60

Navigating the Website *61*

Question: How do I access Ancestry.com and start navigating the website? 61

Question: I see different tabs on the Ancestry.com homepage. What are they for, and which ones should I explore first? 61

Question: I'm new to genealogy, and the website seems overwhelming. Is there a guided tour or tutorial for beginners? 62

Question: I want to search for specific records or ancestors. How do I conduct an effective search on Ancestry.com? 62

Question: I see that there are millions of records on Ancestry.com. How can I narrow down my search to find my specific ancestors more easily? 63

Question: I'm looking for specific records, such as census data or birth certificates. How do I access these records on Ancestry.com? 63

Question: I've found an interesting record, but it's in a different language. Is there a way to translate it into English? 63

Question: I'm curious about my ancestor's hometown and historical context. How do I find additional information about a specific location? 64

Question: The website mentions a "Research Wiki" and a "Learning Center." How can I access these valuable resources? 64

Question: How can the Ancestry.com Research Wiki help me in my genealogy research? 64

Question: I'd like to see what other users are discussing and share my discoveries. How can I join the Ancestry.com community? 65

Question: How can I share my research findings and stories with others in the Ancestry.com Community? 67

Question: How can I find and read stories shared by other researchers in the Ancestry.com Community? 68

Question: Can I comment on stories shared by others in the Ancestry.com Community? 68

Question: How can I show appreciation for a story that I find particularly interesting or helpful? 69

Question: What should I include in my research findings or stories to make them more engaging? 69

Question: How can I ensure the accuracy of the information I share in my research stories? 70

Question: Can I edit or update a story after I've posted it?.....................70

Question: How can I get feedback on my research findings or stories from the Ancestry.com Community?...71

Question: Is there a way to organize and categorize the stories I share on Ancestry.com?...71

Additional Resources:...71

Chapter 3.. 73

Building Your Family Tree.. 73

Adding Yourself and Your Immediate Family.................. 73

Question: How do I add myself to the family tree on Ancestry.com? 73

Question: Can I add my immediate family members to the family tree as well? 74

Question: What if I don't have all the information for my immediate family members?..74

Question: Can I share photos and documents along with my research stories on Ancestry.com? 75

Question: How can I include family photos and documents for each family member? 75

Question: Can I create a separate section to document family traditions and cultural heritage? 76

Question: Can I add deceased family members to the family tree?........76

Exploring Ancestral Lines 77

Question: How do I connect myself to ancestors beyond my immediate family?...77

Question: Can I link media and sources to individuals for whom I only have limited information?...77

Question: Can I link media and sources to individuals from my extended family or collateral lines? 78

Question: Can I link media and sources to individuals who have living descendants in my family tree? 79

Question: Can I link media and sources to individuals from different generations in my family tree? 79

Question: Can I link media and sources to individuals for whom I have DNA test results? 80

Question: How do I ensure that the linked media and sources are accurate and relevant to the individual? 80

Question: Can I link media and sources to individuals from different branches of my family tree? 81

Question: Can I link media and sources to individuals who were part of historical events or lived in significant periods? 81

Question: Can I add family members who have passed away, even if I didn't know them personally? 82

Question: How do I begin exploring my ancestral lines on Ancestry.com? 82

Question: What are the essential details I should include when adding an ancestor to my family tree? 83

Attach photos and relevant documents* *83

Question: Can I search for historical records related to my family members on Ancestry.com? 83

Question: How can I ensure the accuracy of the information I add to my family tree? 84

Question: What should I do if I encounter conflicting information about an ancestor? 84

Question: How can I extend my ancestral lines beyond the immediate family? 84

Question: What do I do if I encounter a gap in my ancestral lines with limited available records? 85

Merging Duplicate Records* *85

Question: How can I merge duplicate records on Ancestry.com? 85

Question: What should I do if the records contain duplicate parents, spouses, or children during the merge? 87

Question: How do I merge duplicate records of the same ancestor in my family tree? 87

Question: What are duplicate records in Family Tree, and why is it essential to merge them? 88

Question: How can I identify possible duplicate records in Family Tree? 88

Question: What should I do if I am uncertain whether two records are duplicates? 88

Question: How can I merge duplicate records on the Ancestry.com website? 89

Question: How can I merge duplicate records using the Family Tree mobile app? 89

Question: Can I undo a merge if I made a mistake? 90

Question: What information should I compare before deciding which record to keep in a merge? 90

Question: How do I decide which record to keep when merging if there are differences between the records? 91

Question: How can I replace information on the right with information from the left during the merge? 91

Question: What do I need to do after completing the merge? 92

Question: Why do merges fail in Family Tree, and how can I avoid merge failures? 92

Question: Can I merge duplicates using Family Tree Lite? 92

Question: Where can I find related articles and additional help about merging duplicates in Family Tree? 93

Collaborating with Family Members 93

Question: Why is collaborating with family members essential when building your family tree? 93

Question: How can I collaborate with other family members to fill gaps in my ancestral lines? 94

Question: Can I invite my family members to collaborate on our family tree? 94

Question: How can I involve family members in the process of building our family tree? 95

Question: What are the benefits of creating a private family group on Ancestry.com for collaboration? 95

Question: How can I encourage family members to participate actively in the family tree-building process?...96

Question: *What are some effective ways to divide research tasks among family members to maximize efficiency?* 96

Question: How can we verify the accuracy of information shared by different family members during collaboration? 97

Question: Are there any tools or features on Ancestry.com that facilitate collaboration among family members? 97

Question: How can we handle disagreements or conflicting information among family members during collaboration? 99

Question: What role does storytelling play in collaborating with family members? 99

Question: How can we encourage older family members to share their oral history and experiences? 100

Question: What steps can we take to preserve family traditions and cultural practices during collaboration?...100

Question: How can we ensure that all family members have equal access to the collaborative efforts and information on Ancestry.com? 101

Question: What are some creative ways to engage younger family members in the family tree-building process? 101

Question: What guidelines should we establish to maintain data privacy and security while collaborating online? 104

Question: How can we celebrate milestones and achievements in the collaborative journey of building our family tree?................................104

Additional Resources:..104

Chapter 4*.. *107

Searching and Accessing Records*......................... *107

How to Conduct Effective Searches *107*

Question: How can I ensure my research is accurate and well-documented? 107

Question: What strategies can I use to break through brick walls with difficult ancestors? 108

Question: How do I access census data and vital records on Ancestry.com for my ancestors? 109

Question: How can I make the most of census data for my genealogy research? 109

Question: Can I access census data and vital records from different countries on Ancestry.com? 110

Question: How can I verify the accuracy of vital records found on Ancestry.com? 110

Question: What resources can I use on Ancestry.com to learn more about genealogy research? 111

Question: What strategies can I use to research ancestors from different countries or cultures? 112

Question: What are some general tips for conducting effective searches on Ancestry.com? 113

Question: What strategies can I employ to overcome common challenges in finding ancestors with common names? 113

Question: What should I do if my initial search does not yield any relevant results? 113

Question: How can I make the most of the search suggestions and related records feature on Ancestry.com? 114

Question: How can I conduct searches in specific record collections or databases on Ancestry.com? 114

Question: What is the best approach to searching for ancestors with common name variations due to cultural or linguistic differences? 114

Question: How can I effectively search for female ancestors whose names might have changed due to marriage? 115

Question: What strategies can I use to search for ancestors with limited information, such as missing birth dates or locations? 115

Question: What can I do if I encounter language barriers while searching for records in foreign countries? 115

Question: How can I verify the authenticity and accuracy of records found during my searches? 116

Question: What resources and reference materials can I consult to improve my search skills and techniques? 116

Question: How can I overcome challenges and roadblocks in my research? 116

Utilizing Filters and Advanced Search Options************ 118**

Question: How can I use the date range filter to narrow down search results to a specific time period? 118

Question: How can I effectively use the record type filter to search for specific types of records, like census or immigration records? 118

Question: What is the benefit of using the collection filter, and how can it help me search within specific record collections? 118

Question: What is the purpose of the place filter, and how can it help in finding records about my ancestors in a particular location? 119

Question: How can I use the "Any Event" filter to broaden my search and explore records that may not have specific event dates or locations? .. 119

Question: What are some advanced search options, and how can I use them to refine my search further? 120

Question: How can I utilize wildcards and fuzzy search to find records with similar spellings or variations of names? 120

Question: How can I use search operators (e.g., AND, OR, NOT) to create more complex and targeted searches? 120

Question: What are some best practices for using search operators like AND, OR, and NOT? 121

Question: How can I use the Soundex feature to find records with similar-sounding names? 121

Question: How can I efficiently use the "Exact" search option to find records with names that match exactly? 123

Question: How do I use the "Keyword" search option to explore records based on specific keywords or phrases? 123

Question: Can I combine filters and advanced search options to conduct highly targeted searches? 124

Question: What strategies can I employ to adjust filters and search options if my initial search does not yield relevant results? 124

Question: How can I save and reuse search filters for future searches?124

Question: Are there additional resources or tutorials available on Ancestry.com to improve my skills in utilizing filters and advanced search options effectively? 125

Accessing Historical Records, Census Data, and Vital Records.. 126

Question: How can I access historical records that are not yet digitized on Ancestry.com? 126

Question: How do I find and add historical records from external sources to my immediate family members' profiles? 127

Question: How can I access historical birth records on Ancestry.com?. 127

Question: What types of vital records are available on Ancestry.com, and how can they assist my research? 128

Question: How can I access and view the full details of census records and vital records on Ancestry.com? 129

Question: Can I download or save census data and vital records from Ancestry.com? 129

Question: Can I access birth, marriage, and death records for free on Ancestry.com? 130

Question: What is census data, and how can they help with my genealogy research? 130

Question: How do I interpret the information in census data and vital records for my research? 130

Question: Can I download or save census data and vital records from Ancestry.com? 131

Question: How can I use census data to learn more about my ancestor's living conditions and family structure? 132

Question: How can I use vital records to trace my ancestor's life events and milestones? 132

Question: How do I find and access specific types of vital records, such as marriage certificates or death records? 133

Question: How do I access historical marriage records to learn about my ancestors' marital unions? 133

Question: Can I access historical death records to find information about my deceased ancestors? 134

Question: How can I access census data from different time periods on Ancestry.com? 134

Question: What types of information can I find in census records on Ancestry.com? 135

Question: How do I access census data from specific countries on Ancestry.com? 135

Question: Can I access census records from different U.S. states on Ancestry.com? 136

Question: How can I access historical immigration records to learn about my ancestors' arrival in a new country? 136

Question: Can I access ship passenger lists on Ancestry.com for my ancestors who immigrated to the United States? 137

Question: How do I access historical military records to find information about my ancestors' military service? 137

Question: Can I access pension records on Ancestry.com to learn about my ancestors' military benefits? 138

Question: How can I access historical naturalization records to find information about my ancestors' path to citizenship? 138

Question: Can I access historical land and property records to trace my ancestors' land ownership and transactions? 139

Question: How do I access church records on Ancestry.com to find information about baptisms, marriages, and burials? 139

Additional Resources: 140

Chapter 5 .... ***141***

Uploading and Managing Documents Photos Etc..141

Preserving Family Photos and Documents ***141***

Question: How can I preserve and share family photos and documents on Ancestry.com? 141

Question: Can I upload media for multiple family members at once? .. 141

Question: How can I link a specific photo or document to a particular individual in my family tree? 142

Question: Are there any restrictions on the file types I can upload? 143

Question: How can I ensure the photos/documents I upload are preserved for the long term? 143

Question: Is there a limit to the number of photos/documents I can upload? 144

Question: Can I add descriptions or captions to the photos/documents I upload? 144

Question: Can I share the photos/documents I upload with other family members? 145

Question: Is there a way to organize my uploaded photos/documents? 145

Question: How can I add photos/documents to an existing album? 146

Question: Can I create separate albums for different branches of my family? 146

Question: Can I upload photos/documents that are physically stored in an album or binder? 147

Question: How can I view and manage the photos/documents I've uploaded on Ancestry.com? 147

Question: Can I add photos/documents to my family tree directly from the Ancestry.com mobile app? 148

Question: Are there any privacy settings for the photos/documents I upload? 148

Question: How can I include family photos and documents for each family member? 149

Upload photos, documents and stories *151*

Question: How can I ensure the preservation of family heirlooms and documents?....151

Uploading Media to Ancestry.com.... *151*

Question: How do I upload photos and documents to Ancestry.com? .151

Question: Can I upload photos and documents related to census records on Ancestry.com?....152

Question: How do I upload census data to Ancestry.com?....152

Question: Can I upload vital records such as birth certificates and death certificates to Ancestry.com?....153

Question: How do I attach vital records to individuals in my family tree on Ancestry.com?....153

Question: Is there a limit to the number of photos and documents I can upload on Ancestry.com?....154

Question: Can I upload photos and documents from my mobile device to Ancestry.com?....154

Question: Can I upload scanned images of historical photos to Ancestry.com?....154

Question: Can I upload documents written in languages other than English to Ancestry.com? 155

Question: Can I upload audio recordings or oral histories to Ancestry.com?....155

Question: How do I ensure that my uploaded photos and documents are private or only accessible to specific family members?....156

Question: Can I upload media that contains sensitive or private information about living individuals? 157

Question: Can I upload videos or home movies to Ancestry.com? 157

Question: Can I upload media from social media platforms to Ancestry.com? 157

Question: Can I upload media for multiple family members at once? ..158

Question: How can I link a specific photo or document to a particular individual in my family tree? 158

Question: Are there any restrictions on the file types I can upload? 159

Question: How can I ensure the photos/documents I upload are preserved for the long term? 159

Question: Is there a limit to the number of photos/documents I can upload? 160

Question: Can I add descriptions or captions to the photos/documents I upload? 160

Question: Can I share the photos/documents I upload with other family members? 161

Question: Is there a way to organize my uploaded photos/documents? 161

Question: How can I add photos/documents to an existing album? 161

Question: Can I create separate albums for different branches of my family? 162

Question: Can I upload photos/documents that are physically stored in an album or binder? 162

Question: How can I view and manage the photos/documents I've uploaded on Ancestry.com? 163

Question: Can I add photos/documents to my family tree directly from the Ancestry.com mobile app? 163

Question: Are there any privacy settings for the photos/documents I upload? 164

Linking Media to Specific Individuals or Events............ 164

Question: How do I ensure that the uploaded media is properly linked to individuals in my family tree? 164

Question: Can I upload media for ancestors who lived in different time periods, such as the 18th or 19th century? 165

Question: Can I create a timeline of media for a specific individual in the family tree? 165

Question: Can I upload media for family members who were part of historical events or lived in significant periods? 166

Question: Can I upload media related to family traditions and cultural practices? 166

Question: Can I upload media for adopted family members or those related through marriage? 166

Question: Can I upload media for family members who emigrated from one country to another? 167

Question: Can I upload media for family members who served in the military or participated in wars? 167

Question: Can I upload media for family members who were involved in historical movements or social causes? 167

Question: Can I upload media for family members who were pioneers or early settlers in a particular region? 168

Question: Can I upload media for family members who were artists, writers, or musicians? 168

Question: How do I link media to specific individuals in my family tree on Ancestry.com? 168

Question: Can I link multiple photos or documents to one individual in my family tree? 169

Question: How do I remove or unlink media from an individual's profile on Ancestry.com? 169

Question: Can I link media to multiple individuals in my family tree? ...169

Question: Can I link census data and vital records to specific individuals in my family tree? 170

Question: How do I link census data and vital records to individuals in my family tree on Ancestry.com? 170

Question: Can I link media and sources to the same individual in my family tree? 171

Question: Can I link memories to specific events or dates in the family tree? 171

Question: Can I see who has viewed or interacted with the memories I've uploaded? 171

Question: Can I add memories to individuals who are not directly related to my family tree? 172

Question: How can I share memories with family members who are not on Ancestry.com?..172

Question: Can I import memories from other platforms or family history websites into Ancestry.com?..172

Question: Can I add memories to individuals who have not been added to the family tree yet?...173

Question: How can I ensure the privacy and security of the memories I upload on Ancestry.com?...173

Additional Resources:..174

Chapter 6.. 175

Research Tips and Strategies.................................. 175

Researching Difficult Ancestors.......................................175

Question: How do I research difficult ancestors on Ancestry.com? 175

Question: What should I do if I can't find any records for a difficult ancestor on Ancestry.com?...176

Question: Are there any specialized resources or databases that can aid in exploring specific ancestral lines, such as Native American or African American heritage?..177

Question: What strategies can I employ when researching ancestors with common surnames or limited identifying information?........................177

Question: Are there any specialized resources or databases that can aid in exploring specific ancestral lines, such as Native American or African American heritage? 178

Using Ancestry Wiki and Learning Center 178

Question: What are the benefits of utilizing Ancestry.com Wiki and Learning Center in exploring ancestral lines? 178

Question: What is the Ancestry.com Wiki, and how can I use it for my genealogy research? 179

Question: What is the Ancestry.com Learning Center, and how can it help me with my genealogy research? 180

Question: How can I use the Ancestry.com Wiki to research a specific location for my ancestor's records? 180

Question: What type of information can I find in the Ancestry.com Wiki for a specific location? 181

Question: How do I access courses and webinars in the Ancestry.com Learning Center? 181

Question: How can the Ancestry.com Learning Center help me improve my genealogy research skills? 182

Leveraging Community and Online Forums 183

Question: How can I leverage community and online forums to aid in my exploration of ancestral lines? 183

Question: How can I use Ancestry.com Wiki and Learning Center to research difficult ancestors? 183

Question: How can I leverage community and online forums to research difficult ancestors? 184

Question: What are community and online forums, and how can they help with my genealogy research? 185

Question: How do I find and join genealogy groups and forums on Ancestry.com? 185

Question: How can I benefit from participating in genealogy forums? . 186

Question: What etiquettes should I follow while participating in genealogy forums? 186

Question: How can I search for specific topics or surnames within genealogy forums? 187

Question: What should I do if I can't find an answer to my research question in the genealogy forums? 187

Question: How can I contribute my knowledge and research findings to genealogy forums? 188

Question: Can I share images or documents in genealogy forums to support my research? 188

Question: Can I communicate privately with other members in genealogy forums? 189

Question: How can I keep track of forum discussions that interest me? 189

Question: Can I interact with forum members from different countries or regions? 189

Question: Are there forum discussions specifically for beginners in genealogy research? 190

Additional Resources: 190

Chapter 7 192

Collaborating in Ancestry Community 192

Joining Ancestry Groups 192

Question: Why should I consider joining Ancestry.com groups? 192

Question: Can I join more than one Ancestry.com group? 193

Question: How do I find Ancestry.com groups that are relevant to my research? 193

Question: What kind of discussions happen in Ancestry.com groups? 194

Question: How do I actively participate in group discussions? 194

Question: Can I ask for help with my specific genealogy challenges in a group? 195

Question: How can I make sure I'm following the group's guidelines and being respectful?....195

Question: Can I leave a group if I'm no longer interested?....196

Question: How do I receive notifications from the groups I've joined?.196

Question: Can I invite others to join an Ancestry.com group?....196

Question: How can I ask questions about my genealogy research in the Ancestry.com Community?....197

Question: How can I answer questions in the Ancestry.com Community?....197

Question: Can I ask for help with specific individuals or family lines in the Ancestry.com Community?....198

Question: How do I search for questions related to my research interests?....198

Question: What should I do if I come across a question that I can answer?....199

Question: Can I provide additional information or clarification to an existing answer?....199

Question: How can I make sure my answer is accurate before posting it?....200

Question: What if I don't know the answer to a question?....200

Question: Can I receive notifications when someone answers my question?....201

Question: How do I mark a question as "answered"?....201

Question: What if I want to follow up on a question I asked earlier?....202

Sharing Research Findings and Stories.... 202

Question: How can I share my family history discoveries with others?.202

Question: Can I share photos and documents along with my research stories on Ancestry.com?....204

Question: How can I find and read stories shared by other researchers in the Ancestry.com Community?....204

Question: Can I comment on stories shared by others in the Ancestry.com Community? 205

Question: How can I show appreciation for a story that I find particularly interesting or helpful? 205

Question: What should I include in my research findings or stories to make them more engaging? 206

Question: How can I ensure the accuracy of the information I share in my research stories? 206

Question: Can I edit or update a story after I've posted it? 207

Question: How can I get feedback on my research findings or stories from the Ancestry.com Community? 207

Question: Is there a way to organize and categorize the stories I share on Ancestry.com? 208

Additional Resources: 208

Chapter 8 210

Advanced Features and DNA Testing 210

Exploring Advanced Ancestry Features 210

Question: What are some advanced features on Ancestry.com that I can explore to enhance my genealogy research? 210

Question: How do I use Record Hints on Ancestry.com to discover new information about my ancestors? 211

Question: What is the Ancestry.com Catalog, and how can it assist me in my research? 211

Question: How can the Family Tree app help me manage my family tree while I'm on the go? 212

Question: How can I access online genealogy classes on Ancestry.com? 212

Question: Can I access the Ancestry.com Learning Center courses anytime, or are they scheduled? 213

Question: How can I benefit from the insights and experiences of other genealogists in the Ancestry.com community? 213

Question: What are some topics I can explore in the Ancestry.com Community forum? 214

Integrating DNA Testing with Your Family History 214

Question: How can I integrate DNA testing with my family history research on Ancestry.com? 214

Question: What is the benefit of integrating DNA testing with my Ancestry.com family tree? 215

Question: How do I link my DNA test results to my Ancestry.com account? 215

Question: How do I identify shared ancestors with my DNA matches on Ancestry.com? 216

Question: Can I communicate with my DNA matches on Ancestry.com? 216

Question: How do I send a message to my DNA matches on Ancestry.com? 217

Question: Can DNA testing help me break through genealogical brick walls? 217

Question: How do I ensure privacy when integrating DNA testing with my Ancestry.com family tree? 218

Question: Can I upload DNA test results from other testing companies to Ancestry.com? 218

Question: How can I leverage DNA testing to enhance my exploration of ancestral lines? 219

Understanding Genetic Genealogy 219

Question: How can I integrate DNA testing with my family history research on Ancestry.com? .... **Error! Bookmark not defined.**

Question: What is the benefit of integrating DNA testing with my Ancestry.com family tree? .... **Error! Bookmark not defined.**

Question: How do I link my DNA test results to my Ancestry.com account?... **Error! Bookmark not defined.**

Question: How do I identify shared ancestors with my DNA matches on Ancestry.com?..219

Question: Can I communicate with my DNA matches on Ancestry.com? 220

Question: How do I send a message to my DNA matches on Ancestry.com?..221

Question: Can DNA testing help me break through genealogical brick walls?..222

Question: How do I ensure privacy when integrating DNA testing with my Ancestry.com family tree?..222

Question: Can I upload DNA test results from other testing companies to Ancestry.com?..223

Question: What is genetic genealogy and how can it enhance my family history research?..224

Question: How does genetic genealogy work on Ancestry.com?..........225

Question: What is the Shared Ancestor Hints feature on Ancestry.com DNA? 226

Question: Can genetic genealogy help me find relatives from different parts of the world?...227

Question: How do I interpret DNA match information on Ancestry.com? 228

Question: Can I explore my genetic ethnicity on Ancestry.com?...........229

Question: How can I use genetic genealogy to confirm relationships? .230

Question: What should I do if I find a potential relative through genetic genealogy? 231

Question: Can I use genetic genealogy to trace my lineage back through many generations?..233

Question: How can I learn more about genetic genealogy and its applications? 234

Chapter 9 .... *236*

Ensuring Data Security and Privacy *236*

Best Practices for Securing Personal Data *236*

Question: How does Ancestry.com ensure the accuracy of its information? 236

Question: Are there any privacy concerns associated with using Ancestry.com? 237

Question: What are some basic best practices for securing my Ancestry.com account? 237

Additional Resources: 238

Question: How can I create a strong and secure password for my Ancestry.com account? 238

Question: What is two-factor authentication (FA), and why should I enable it? 239

Question: How do I enable two-factor authentication (FA) for my Ancestry.com account? 240

Question: Is it safe to use public Wi-Fi when accessing Ancestry.com? 240

Question: How can I protect my personal data when sharing it with other family members on Ancestry.com? 241

Question: What should I do if I suspect unauthorized access to my Ancestry.com account? 242

Question: Can I delete my Ancestry.com account if I no longer want to use the platform? 242

Question: How can I ensure the security of physical documents and photos I upload to Ancestry.com? 243

Question: What should I do if I encounter suspicious or phishing emails related to Ancestry.com? 244

Question: Can I share my Ancestry.com login credentials with others? 244

Understanding Ancestry.com's Privacy Policies *245*

Question: Why is data security important when using Ancestry.com? .245

Question: What resources are available to help me understand and implement data security best practices on Ancestry.com? 246

Question: What are Ancestry.com's privacy policies, and why are they important? 246

Question: How does Ancestry.com handle the personal information I provide? 247

Question: Can I control who can access my family history information on Ancestry.com?...248

Question: What information is considered public on Ancestry.com?....248

Question: How can I make my family history information more private on Ancestry.com?...249

Question: Will my uploaded photos and documents be visible to the public on Ancestry.com? 249

Question: Can I control who can edit and contribute to my family history information?..250

Question: How does Ancestry.com protect my data from unauthorized access? 250

Question: Does Ancestry.com share my data with third parties?..........251

Question: How does Ancestry.com use cookies and tracking technologies?..251

Question: Can I opt out of receiving emails and notifications from Ancestry.com?...251

Question: How can I request access to or correction of my personal information on Ancestry.com?...252

Question: What should I do if I have concerns or questions about Ancestry.com's privacy policies?..252

Additional Resources:...253

Other Books Available on Amazon

Liahona Publications

Sudoku Puzzles

Sudoku Bliss for All Ages:
Dive into the world of Sudoku
with our puzzle book

Notary Public Logbook

** 8.5 x 11 & 6 x 9 Paperback **

Our Notary Public Logbook is your key,
to efficient and precise
record-keeping.

The Magic of Enchanted Adventures

*** E-Book & PaperBack***

A series that takes readers on a
journey through a magical world
filled with wonder, excitement.

FamilySearch FAQ

** E-Book & PaperBack **

Discover the secrets of unveiling
your family's history with
an ultimate guide to genealogy.

Chapter 1
Introduction to Ancestry.com

What is Ancestry and Family History?

Question: Can I collaborate with my family members on our family tree?

Answer: *Absolutely! Ancestry.com offers collaboration features like Family Groups and Member Connect. Check out Ancestry Support for guidance on collaborating with family members to enrich your family tree collectively.*

Ancestry Support

Question: What are some creative ways to preserve my ancestral journey?

Answer: *Explore creative options to preserve your family history, such as creating a Family*

History Kit with taped interviews and digitized music, as suggested by Senior Living Activity

Question: Any ideas for creative family history-themed crafts or DIY projects?

Answer: *Inject a personal touch into your family history project with creative crafts. Explore ideas from Sixty and Me for preserving family history through DIY projects. Whether it's a handmade family tree or a memory scrapbook, these crafts add a unique flair to your project.*

Different Forms of Family History (e.g., books, albums, newsletters)

Question: How can I start a family newsletter that engages readers?

Answer: *Starting a family newsletter is a fantastic idea! Craft engaging content, share exciting discoveries from your family history journey, and use platforms like Ancestry.com to connect with relatives. Follow your creativity, and your newsletter will become a cherished family tradition.*

Question: I'm not tech-savvy, but I want to create a family history book. Where do I begin?

Answer: *Embarking on a family history book is simpler than it seems. Begin with basic tools on Ancestry.com, and gradually explore more advanced features as you become comfortable. Utilize resources like Family Tree Magazine's Tips and Tricks for Beginners for guidance tailored to beginners.*

Question: How can I incorporate our family's traditions into the project?

Answer: *Preserving traditions is a beautiful aspect of family history. Blend traditional elements with Ancestry.com's multimedia capabilities. Document rituals, stories, or recipes, and add them to your family tree. This adds a personal touch that future generations will cherish.*

Question: How can I create a dynamic multimedia presentation for my family?

Answer: *Crafting a dynamic presentation is exciting! Use multimedia features on Ancestry.com to incorporate photos, documents, and stories. Check YouTube for tutorials on fixing duplicates and enhancing your presentation skills.*

Question: Are there online platforms for creating a digital family archive?

Answer: *Ancestry.com itself serves as an excellent platform for creating a digital family archive. Utilize its features to organize documents, photos, and stories. Your family can access this archive easily, fostering a sense of connection across generations.*

Benefits of Creating a Family History

Question: What are the benefits of undertaking this family history journey?

Answer: *Embarking on a family history journey is not just about names and dates. It's a fascinating exploration that connects you to your roots, fostering a deeper understanding of your identity, heritage, and familial bonds. The journey itself becomes a source of joy and discovery.*

Question: How can family history positively impact relationships with living family members?

Answer: *Sharing family history findings can strengthen relationships. It creates meaningful conversations, builds a sense of unity, and allows you to appreciate each other's unique stories. It's a journey that brings family members closer together.*

Question: What are the emotional benefits of delving into family history?

Answer: *Delving into family history provides a profound emotional experience. It can evoke a sense of belonging, pride, and understanding. Discovering the stories of resilience and triumph within your family tree can be a deeply moving and enriching process.*

Question: How can knowing my family history improve my overall well-being?

Answer: *Knowing your family history contributes to a sense of identity, purpose, and resilience. It can provide a foundation for self-discovery, helping you navigate life's challenges with a deeper understanding of your roots.*

Question: Positive influence on children's interest in heritage:

Answer: *Creating a family history project can significantly impact your children's interest in their heritage:*

1. ***Educational Value:*** *Present the project as an exciting educational adventure,*

introducing them to history, geography, and cultural diversity through their own family's story.

2. ***Storytelling:*** *Share captivating stories about ancestors, making history more relatable and engaging for children.*
3. ***Interactive Learning:*** *Involve children in the process—let them help with research, interviews, or even creative aspects like designing a family tree.*
4. ***Pride and Identity:*** *Learning about their roots fosters a sense of pride and identity, connecting them to a broader cultural context.*
5. ***Family Bonding:*** *The project becomes a shared family experience, strengthening bonds and creating lasting memories.*

By framing the family history journey as an enriching and enjoyable experience, you can ignite your children's curiosity about their heritage.

When to Start Your Family History Journey

Question: How do I start preserving our family's stories?

Answer: *Begin by gathering anecdotes, photos, and documents. Organize them on Ancestry.com, creating a structured family tree. Start small, focus on a specific branch, and gradually expand. Documenting family stories becomes an enjoyable journey of discovery.*

Question: How can I document my family's history digitally without feeling overwhelmed?

Answer: *Start with Ancestry.com's user-friendly tools. Input basic information, gradually adding more details. Explore tutorials like AncestryDNA ThruLines Tips and Strategies for guidance. The key is to take small steps, celebrating each achievement, and enjoying the digital documentation process.*

Question: Concerns about the cost of creating a family history:

Answer: *Creating a family history doesn't have to break the bank. Explore budget-friendly options:*

1. ***Utilize Free Resources:*** *Leverage free genealogy platforms like Ancestry to access basic records and start your journey at no cost.*
2. ***Public Libraries:*** *Visit local libraries where you can access archives, books, and resources without spending money.*
3. ***FamilySearch Centers:*** *The Church of Jesus Christ of Latter-day Saints provides free Genealogy Research help in over 4600 locations worldwide and in over 126 counties. This service is provided free of charge from volunteers worldwide and includes many online services such as Ancestry, Local Newspapers and many more.*
4. ***DIY Projects:*** *Engage in creative DIY projects for family history, like scrapbooking or creating a digital family tree. These activities often require minimal expenses.*

5. ***Collaborative Effort:*** *Involve family members to share the workload and costs. Collaborative efforts can make the project more affordable and enjoyable.*
6. ***Online Tutorials:*** *Explore online tutorials and tips to make the most of free or cost-effective features on genealogy platforms.*

Remember, the journey itself is valuable, and you can tailor it to fit your budget.

Additional Resources:

1. *Sixty and Me - 7 Ideas for Preserving Your Family History*
2. *Ancestry® | Family Tree, Genealogy & Family History Records*
3. *8 Ways to Preserve Your Family History*

Quick Links

Chapter 2

Getting Started on Ancestry.com

Overview of Available Features and Tools

Question: What are the main benefits of using Ancestry.com for ancestry research?

Answer: *Ancestry.com offers several key benefits for researchers, including:*

Access to a vast collection of historical records: Ancestry boasts a massive database of historical documents, including census records, birth certificates, marriage licenses, obituaries, military records, and more.

This allows researchers to trace their family history across generations and uncover valuable information about their ancestors' lives.

***DNA testing**: AncestryDNA, offered by Ancestry.com, provides insights into your ethnicity and connects you with potential genetic relatives. This can be a powerful tool for breaking down brick walls in your research and discovering new branches of your family tree.*

***Collaboration tools:** Ancestry.com offers features like family trees, shared documents, and messaging boards that allow you to collaborate with other researchers and share your findings. This can be especially helpful for those researching common ancestors or families with complex histories.*

***Expert resources and guidance:** Ancestry.com provides access to a wealth of learning materials, including articles, webinars, and podcasts, as well as expert advice from genealogists. This can help you learn best practices for research, overcome challenges, and make the most of the platform's features.*

***Discoveries and unexpected connections:** Ancestry.com's algorithms can help you discover surprising connections and hidden stories within your family history. This can lead to a deeper understanding of your* *ancestors and their lives, making your research journey even more rewarding.*

Question: Is Ancestry.com suitable for beginners?

Answer: *Yes, Ancestry.com is a user-friendly platform suitable for both beginners and experienced researchers. The website offers a range of tools and resources to help you get started, including tutorials, guides, and a searchable help center. Additionally, AncestryDNA provides clear instructions and explanations for understanding your DNA results.*

Question: What are the costs associated with using Ancestry.com?

Answer: *Ancestry.com offers free basic membership that allows you to search some records and build a family tree. However, to access most historical documents, utilize DNA testing, and enjoy advanced features, a paid subscription is required. There are different* *subscription plans available, each offering varying levels of access and features.*

Question: Tell me what tools and features on can help me discover my family history?

Answer: *Several tools on Ancestry.com can aid in your family history journey:*

Search historical records: *Use the search engine to find specific records, such as birth certificates, census records, and immigration documents. Filter your search by location, date, and other criteria to narrow down your results.*

Build a family tree: *Create a visual representation of your family history, adding information about your ancestors and their relationships. Ancestry.com can suggest potential matches based on records and DNA connections.*

Explore Hints: *Ancestry.com provides personalized hints based on your family tree and research activity. These hints can point* *you towards new records, potential relatives, and information gaps in your research.*

Connect with DNA relatives: *Discover genetic relatives through AncestryDNA and learn about your shared ancestry. This can lead to exciting discoveries and expand your understanding of your family tree.*

Research communities: *Join online communities and forums focused on specific regions, surnames, or historical events. These communities provide valuable resources and opportunities to connect with other researchers and share information.*

Question: What are the main features and tools available on Ancestry.com?

Answer: *Ancestry.com offers a comprehensive suite of features and tools designed to assist you in your ancestry research. Here are some of the key ones:*

Search Records: *Access billions of historical records, including birth certificates, census records, marriage licenses, obituaries, military records, and immigration documents.*

You can search by name, date, location, and other criteria.

Family Tree Builder: *Create a visual representation of your family tree, adding information about your ancestors and their relationships. Ancestry.com can suggest potential matches based on records and DNA connections.*

DNA Testing: *Unlock insights into your ethnicity, heritage, and potential genetic relatives through AncestryDNA. You can connect with others who share your DNA and learn about your shared ancestry.*

Hints: *Receive personalized suggestions based on your existing research, highlighting potential new avenues for exploration and records you may have missed.*

Collaboration Tools: *Share your family tree, documents, and photos with other researchers, collaborate on projects, and discuss discoveries.*

Learning Resources: *Explore a vast collection of articles, tutorials, webinars, and podcasts covering various genealogy topics,* *from beginner basics to advanced research techniques.*

Research Guides: *Find tailored advice and resources for specific research areas, such as African American genealogy, immigration records, or military records.*

Expert Q&A: *Get your research questions answered by experienced genealogists during scheduled Q&A sessions.*

Help Center*: Access a searchable database of articles and FAQs covering common research challenges and solutions.*

Online Communities: *Connect with other researchers facing similar challenges or researching specific regions, surnames, or historical events.*

Storytelling Tools: *Add narratives, photos, and timelines to your family tree, making your discoveries more engaging and meaningful for others.*

Blog Platform: *Share your research journey, discoveries, and insights with a wider audience, contributing to the genealogy community.*

Question: What are some of the unique features that set Ancestry.com apart?

Answer: *Ancestry.com boasts several unique features that differentiate it from other genealogy platforms:*

The Largest Collection of Records: *With billions of historical records spanning various regions and eras, Ancestry.com offers unparalleled access to historical information.*

DNA Insights: *AncestryDNA provides detailed ethnicity estimates, identifies potential genetic relatives, and offers tools to explore your shared ancestry.*

ThruLines: *This unique feature helps you break down brick walls in your research by identifying potential ancestor connections based on shared DNA segments and historical records.*

World Explorer: *This subscription plan allows you to access records from around the globe, expanding your research possibilities beyond specific regions.*

Advanced Search Filters: *Refine your search queries with precise filters based on date* *range, location, record type, and other criteria for targeted research.*

Collaboration Features: *Share your research with family members and other researchers, collaborate on projects, and discuss discoveries through messaging boards and shared documents.*

Creating an Account, Paid and Free

Question: What are the different subscription plans and their benefits?

Answer: *Ancestry.com offers several subscription plans with varying levels of access and features:*

Basic (Free): *Limited access to records, family tree building tools, and learning resources.*

World Explorer: *Access billions of records worldwide, including census data, birth certificates, and immigration documents.*

All Access: *Provides the most comprehensive experience, including all features of the World*

Explorer plan, DNA testing, and advanced search filters.

Family Plans: *Share your subscription with family members, allowing them to access the same features and collaborate on research projects.*

Question: What are the pros and cons of using a paid account on Ancestry.com?

Pros:

- *Extensive collection of historical records*
- *DNA testing with detailed insights*
- *Powerful search filters and tools*
- *Collaboration features and online communities*
- *Rich learning*
- *profile picture*
- *Rich learning resources and guides*
- *Unique features like ThruLines and World Explorer*
- *User-friendly platform with helpful tutorials*

Free basic plan *allows exploration and initial research.*

Cons:

- *Subscription fees can be expensive.*
- *Access to advanced features and records requires a paid plan.*
- *Potential for inaccuracies in historical records*
- *DNA testing may not reveal unexpected connections.*
- *Privacy concerns regarding personal information and DNA data*
- *Learning curve for beginners to navigate the platform and research techniques.*

Overall:

Ancestry.com is a powerful tool for researching your family history, offering a vast collection of records, DNA testing, and advanced features. However, its use comes with subscription fees and privacy concerns. Consider your research goals, budget, and comfort level with technology before deciding if Ancestry.com is right for you.

Question: How can I get started with Ancestry.com?

Answer: *Getting started with Ancestry.com is simple and straightforward:*

Create a free account*: Sign up for a free account to explore the platform's basic features and access some historical records.*

Build your family tree: *Start adding information about your ancestors, including names, birthdates, death dates, and relationships.*

Search historical records: *Explore the vast collection of records using the search engine and filters.*

Consider DNA testing: *Unlock deeper insights into your ethnicity and discover potential genetic relatives with AncestryDNA.*

Explore learning resources: *Utilize the platform's articles, tutorials, and webinars to learn more about genealogy research and best practices.*

Seek help and support: *Utilize the Help Center, online communities, and expert Q&A*

sessions for assistance with your research questions and challenges.

Question: What are the steps to setup a Free account on Ancestry.com

Answer: *By following these steps, you can easily set up a free Ancestry account and begin your genealogical journey.*

[Step-up Guide - Free Account]

Go to the Ancestry website: ***Ancestry.com.***

Let's Start Free Trial

1. *Click on the "Start Free Trial" button on the homepage.*
2. *Create Account*
3. *Enter your first name, last name, and email address.*
4. *Create a password for your account.*
5. *Agree to Terms*
6. *Agree to the terms and conditions* ***by checking the appropriate boxes.***
7. *Verify Email*
8. *Check your email inbox* ***for a verification*** *message from Ancestry.*

9. *Click on the verification link provided in the email.*
10. *Provide Additional Information*

Complete your profile by providing additional information about yourself.

*** **Now You Can** Explore Free Features*

Question: What are the steps to setup a Paid account on Ancestry.com

Answer: *By following these steps, you'll successfully set up a paid Ancestry account and embark on your journey to discover your family's unique history.*

Step-up Guide - Paid Membership Account

1. *Navigate to Ancestry's Membership Page https://www.ancestry.com/offers/subscribe*
2. *Choose a Membership Plan*
3. *Review Membership Details*
4. *Click "Subscribe" or "Get Started"*
5. *Create an Ancestry Account*

If you don't have an existing Ancestry account, you'll be prompted to create one.

Provide the necessary information, including your email address and a secure password.

6. *Choose a Payment Method*
7. *Enter your payment details to complete the subscription process. Ancestry accepts various payment methods.*
8. *Confirm Your Subscription*
9. *Review your subscription details and ensure they match your preferences.*
10. *Confirm the subscription to initiate the payment process.*
11. *Access Ancestry's Resources*
12. *Once the payment is processed successfully, you'll gain immediate access to Ancestry's extensive genealogical records and features.*
13. *Explore Your Family History*

Start building your family tree, explore historical records, and utilize Ancestry's tools to uncover your genealogical heritage.

***** If you encounter any issues or have questions, visit Ancestry's Support for comprehensive assistance.***

I Have Some Concerns Setting up my account.

Question: What information do I need to provide when creating an Ancestry.com account, and how is my data protected?

Answer: *When creating an Ancestry.com account, you only need a username, email, and password. Ancestry.com takes privacy seriously, employing robust security measures to protect your data. Review their privacy policy for detailed information on data protection.*

Question: I'm not very tech-savvy. Will I need to download any software to create a Ancestry account?

Answer: *No need to worry! Creating a Ancestry account is web-based, requiring no software downloads. Simply visit Ancestry.com, click "Sign In," and follow the account creation prompts.*

Question: Can I create an Ancestry.com account on my mobile device, or do I have to use a computer?

> ***Answer:*** *Absolutely! You can create an Ancestry.com account on your mobile device. Visit the website using your mobile browser, and the user-friendly interface will guide you through the account setup.*

Question: Is it true that Ancestry.com offers its services entirely for free? Are there any hidden costs or subscriptions required?

> ***Answer:*** *While Ancestry.com offers a free account option, some features may require a subscription. They often provide free access to essential resources, allowing you to explore your family tree without hidden costs.*

Question: I'm concerned about my family tree's security. Who can view the information I add to my tree on Ancestry?

> ***Answer:*** *You have control over your family tree's privacy on Ancestry.com. Choose whether to make it private or share with*

specific individuals. This ensures you determine who can view the information.

Question: Can I collaborate with other family members on my Ancestry.com family tree? How does that work?

Answer: *Certainly! Invite family members to join your tree, allowing collaborative contributions. They can add information, photos, and stories, enriching the shared family history experience.*

Question: I'm worried about making mistakes while building my family tree. Can I undo changes or revert to a previous version?

Answer: *No need to fret! Ancestry.com allows you to undo changes and revert to previous versions of your family tree. Simply navigate to the person's profile, click "Tools," and select "View Change History."*

Question: I have physical family documents and photos I'd like to include in my tree. Can I upload them to Ancestry.com?

> ***Answer:*** *Absolutely! Ancestry.com provides a feature to upload and attach physical family documents and photos to your tree. Preserve your family's history digitally by adding these valuable artifacts.*

Question: Where can I find resources or tutorials to help me make the most of the platform?

> ***Answer:*** *Explore Ancestry Academy™, a collection of free video tutorials offering research tips, genealogy insights, and guidance on using DNA tools. Additionally, check Getting Started, Lesson 1: Starting Your Tree for a step-by-step guide.*

Navigating the Website

Question: How do I access Ancestry.com and start navigating the website?

Answer: *To access Ancestry.com, go to www.ancestry.com. Once there, you'll need to sign up for an account. After signing in, explore the homepage tabs, such as Trees, Search, DNA, and Help. Use the Trees tab to create or view your family tree, the Search tab to find records, and the DNA tab for genetic insights. Visit the Ancestry Family History Learning Hub for in-depth tutorials on genealogy research.*

Question: I see different tabs on the Ancestry.com homepage. What are they for, and which ones should I explore first?

Answer: *The homepage tabs include Trees, Search, DNA, and Help. Start with the Trees tab to create or view your family tree. Explore the Search tab to find historical records, the DNA tab for genetic insights, and the Help tab for support and resources. For a beginner-*

friendly guide, check Ancestry.com: Tips and Tricks for Beginners.

Question: I'm new to genealogy, and the website seems overwhelming. Is there a guided tour or tutorial for beginners?

Answer: *Certainly! Ancestry Academy™ provides video tutorials, including Getting Started, Lesson 1: Starting Your Tree. These lessons offer step-by-step guidance for beginners, making the process more manageable.*

Question: I want to search for specific records or ancestors. How do I conduct an effective search on Ancestry.com?

Answer: *Navigate to the Search tab, enter relevant details, and use filters for precision. Check Ancestry.com: Tips and Tricks for Beginners for additional tips on effective searches.*

Question: I see that there are millions of records on Ancestry.com. How can I narrow down my search to find my specific ancestors more easily?

Answer: *Refine your search by adding more specific details, such as birthplaces or years. Utilize filters on the search results page to narrow down the list.*

Question: I'm looking for specific records, such as census data or birth certificates. How do I access these records on Ancestry.com?

Answer: *Use the Search tab, enter relevant information, and filter results by record type. Detailed steps are available in Ancestry.com: Tips and Tricks for Beginners.*

Question: I've found an interesting record, but it's in a different language. Is there a way to translate it into English?

Answer: *Ancestry.com may offer translation features within the record viewer. Additionally, you can use external translation tools for a more detailed translation.*

Question: I'm curious about my ancestor's hometown and historical context. How do I find additional information about a specific location?

> ***Answer:*** *Explore the Ancestry.com Learning Center or Research Wiki to access resources related to specific locations. Ancestry Academy™ provides tutorials on navigating these valuable resources.*

Question: The website mentions a "Research Wiki" and a "Learning Center." How can I access these valuable resources?

> ***Answer:*** *Access the Research Wiki and Learning Center through the Help tab on the Ancestry.com homepage. For an in-depth tutorial, refer to Ancestry Academy™.*

Question: How can the Ancestry.com Research Wiki help me in my genealogy research?

> ***Answer:*** *The Ancestry.com Research Wiki serves as a valuable resource for genealogists. It offers expert insights, research strategies, and tips on navigating Ancestry.com's features. Explore the wiki to enhance your research*

skills, understand record collections, and overcome challenges in tracing your family history.

Question: I'd like to see what other users are discussing and share my discoveries. How can I join the Ancestry.com community?

Answer: *To join the Ancestry.com community and actively participate in discussions, follow these steps:*

1. ***Navigate to the Community Tab:***
   - *Visit the Ancestry.com homepage.*
   - *Look for the "Community" tab in the top navigation menu.*
2. ***Access the Community Section:***
   - *Click on the "Community" tab to enter the community section of Ancestry.com.*
3. ***Create or Sign In to Your Account:***
   - *If you're not already signed in, you may need to sign in to your Ancestry account. If you don't have an account, you can create one for free.*
4. ***Explore Discussion Boards:***

- *Once in the community section, explore different discussion boards relevant to your genealogy interests. You might find boards related to surnames, regions, or specific research topics.*

5. ***Engage in Conversations:***
   - *Click on discussions that interest you.*
   - *Read through posts, and feel free to engage by commenting on existing threads.*
6. ***Start Your Own Discussions:***
   - *Share your discoveries or ask questions by starting your own discussion threads.*
7. ***Utilize Message Boards:***
   - *Ancestry's Message Boards are a great place for interaction. You can find specific boards for surnames, locations, and research methodologies.*
8. ***Check for Updates:***
   - *Regularly check for updates and new discussions to stay connected with the community.*
9. ***Share Experiences:***
   - *Share your genealogical experiences, seek advice, or contribute your knowledge to help others.*

10. Refer to Detailed Instructions:

- *For more detailed instructions on using Ancestry.com Online Family Trees, privacy settings, and sharing discoveries, refer to the dedicated guide titled "Ancestry.com Online Family Trees: Privacy and Sharing."*

By actively participating in the Ancestry.com community, you can connect with fellow researchers, gain valuable insights, and contribute to the collective knowledge of the genealogy community.

Question: How can I share my research findings and stories with others in the Ancestry.com Community?

Answer: *Sharing your research findings and stories is a wonderful way to contribute. Navigate to the community platform, locate the option to create a new post or share a story, and follow the prompts. Include details such as names, dates, and locations to make your story informative and engaging.*

Question: How can I find and read stories shared by other researchers in the Ancestry.com Community?

Answer: *Discovering stories from fellow researchers is simple. Explore the community platform and look for sections like "Stories" or "Shared Findings." Browse through posts or use search functionalities to find captivating narratives that resonate with your research interests.*

Question: Can I comment on stories shared by others in the Ancestry.com Community?

Answer: *Absolutely! Engage with the community by leaving thoughtful comments on stories that pique your interest. Share your insights, ask questions, or express appreciation. Building connections through positive interactions strengthens the collaborative spirit of the community.*

Question: How can I show appreciation for a story that I find particularly interesting or helpful?

> ***Answer:*** *If you come across a story that resonates with you, show appreciation! Look for options like "Like," "Upvote," or "Thumbs Up" near the story. Your acknowledgment not only encourages the storyteller but also fosters a culture of support within the Ancestry.com Community.*

Question: What should I include in my research findings or stories to make them more engaging?

> ***Answer:*** *Craft engaging stories by including vivid details. Share names, dates, and locations, but also delve into the personalities, challenges, and triumphs of your ancestors. Paint a narrative that captivates readers and brings the past to life, making your research findings more compelling.*

Question: How can I ensure the accuracy of the information I share in my research stories?

Answer: *Prioritize accuracy by cross-referencing information with reliable sources. Verify facts, dates, and relationships before sharing. If you're uncertain, seek input from the community. Ensuring accuracy not only upholds the integrity of your story but also contributes to the overall credibility of shared research.*

Question: Can I edit or update a story after I've posted it?

Answer: *Yes, you can refine your stories even after posting. Locate the "Edit" option near your published story and make necessary updates. This flexibility ensures that your narratives remain accurate and reflective of your evolving research.*

Question: How can I get feedback on my research findings or stories from the Ancestry.com Community?

Answer: *Actively seek feedback by encouraging comments and discussions on your posts. Pose specific questions or request input on aspects of your research. Embracing feedback enhances the collaborative nature of the community, fostering a culture of shared learning and improvement.*

Question: Is there a way to organize and categorize the stories I share on Ancestry.com?

Answer: *Organize your stories by utilizing features like tags or categories, if available. This ensures that your contributions are easily searchable and accessible to others interested in similar topics. An organized approach enhances the overall usability of the community platform.*

Additional Resources:

1. *Getting Started, Lesson 1: Starting Your Tree - ancestry.com*

2. *Ancestry Academy™ - ancestry.com*
3. *Creating a Free Ancestry® Account - ancestry.com*
4. *Ancestry.com: Tips and Tricks for Beginners - familytreemagazine.com*
5. *How To Sign Up For Ancestry.com - techboomers.com*
6. *How to Use Ancestry.com - dummies.com*
7. *Ancestry Family History Learning Hub*
8. *Ancestry.com: Tips and Tricks for Beginners*
9. *Your DNA Guide*
10. *Ancestry.com Online Family Trees: Privacy and Sharing*
11. *AncestryDNA® Communities*
12. *Ancestry Terms and Conditions*
13. *Ancestry® Family History Learning Hub*
14. *DNA Surveys FAQs*
15. *AncestryClassroom | Home*

Chapter 3
Building Your Family Tree

<u>*Adding Yourself and Your Immediate Family*</u>

Question: How do I add myself to the family tree on Ancestry.com?

Answer: *Adding yourself to the family tree is a breeze! Follow these simple steps to ensure your family history journey starts with you.*

1. *Log in to your Ancestry.com account.*
2. *Open your family tree.*
3. *Find an individual close to where you want to add yourself.*
4. *Click on the individual and select "Add Relative."*
5. *Choose "Add Yourself."*
6. *Fill in your details and save.*

Question: Can I add my immediate family members to the family tree as well?

Answer: *Absolutely! Your family tree is about everyone you love. Keep adding immediate family members to create a comprehensive picture.*

1. *Repeat the process for each family member.*
2. *Select the appropriate relationship, like parent or sibling.*

Question: What if I don't have all the information for my immediate family members?

Answer: *No worries! Begin with the information you have, and Ancestry hints will help you discover more about your family.*

1. *Start with what you know.*
2. *Ancestry.com provides hints to fill in missing details.*
3. *Update information as you gather more.*

Question: Can I share photos and documents along with my research stories on Ancestry.com?

> ***Answer:*** *Absolutely! Enhance your stories by attaching photos and documents. While sharing your story, look for options like "Attach File" or "Add Photo." Uploading visual elements enriches your narrative, making it more compelling and providing a holistic view of your family history.*

Question: How can I include family photos and documents for each family member?

> ***Answer:*** *Make your family tree vibrant! Adding photos and documents brings your ancestors to life. Share their stories visually.*
>
> 1. *Open a family member's profile.*
> 2. *Go to the "Gallery" section.*
> 3. *Upload photos, documents, and stories*
> 4. *Add captivating stories in the Bio section.*

Question: Can I create a separate section to document family traditions and cultural heritage?

Answer: *Celebrate diversity! Use notes to capture unique family customs.*

1. *Utilize the "Notes" feature on each family member's profile.*
2. *Create a dedicated section in the Bio for traditions.*

Question: Can I add deceased family members to the family tree?

Answer: Remembering loved ones! Deceased family members are an essential part of your family history.

1. *Add them like living family members.*
2. *Mark their status as deceased.*

Question: How do I connect myself to ancestors beyond my immediate family?

Answer: *Branching out! Explore ancestors beyond your immediate family and expand your family tree.*

1. *Research your ancestors using Ancestry hints.*
2. *Add parents and link them to your tree.*

Question: Can I link media and sources to individuals for whom I only have limited information?

Answer: *Absolutely! Even with limited information, you can enrich your family history. To link media and sources:*

1. *Access the individual's profile on Ancestry.com.*
2. *Navigate to the "Gallery" or "Facts" section.*
3. *Choose "Add Media" or "Add a Source" to attach relevant information.*

4. *If linking media, upload photos, documents, or stories related to the individual.*
5. *If linking sources, input any available details, and cite the source.*
6. *Save your additions to ensure the information is linked.*

Question: Can I link media and sources to individuals from my extended family or collateral lines?

Answer: *Absolutely! Broaden your family history by linking media and sources to extended family members:*

1. *Access the profile of the individual in your tree.*
2. *In the "Gallery" or "Facts" section, choose "Add Media" or "Add a Source."*
3. *Upload relevant media or input source details.*
4. *Save the additions to create a comprehensive family history.*

Question: Can I link media and sources to individuals who have living descendants in my family tree?

Answer: *Yes, you can! Safeguard privacy and enhance your family narrative:*

1. *Access the individual's profile.*
2. *Navigate to "Gallery" or "Facts."*
3. *Choose "Add Media" or "Add a Source."*
4. *Upload relevant media or input source details.*
5. *Save your additions, contributing to a rich family history.*

Question: Can I link media and sources to individuals from different generations in my family tree?

Answer: *Absolutely! Connect generations by linking media and sources:*

1. *Visit the individual's profile.*
2. *In the "Gallery" or "Facts" section, choose "Add Media" or "Add a Source."*
3. *Upload media or input source details.*
4. *Save your additions to create a multi-generational family narrative.*

Question: Can I link media and sources to individuals for whom I have DNA test results?

Answer: Certainly! Enhance your genetic discoveries:

1. *Access the person's profile.*
2. *Navigate to "Gallery" or "Facts."*
3. *Choose "Add Media" or "Add a Source."*
4. *Upload relevant media or input source details.*
5. *Save your additions, contributing to a comprehensive genetic family story.*

Question: How do I ensure that the linked media and sources are accurate and relevant to the individual?

Answer: To ensure accuracy:

1. *Cross-reference information with multiple sources.*
2. *Utilize reputable databases and archives.*
3. *Attach media that directly relates to the individual.*
4. *Verify details before saving additions.*

5. *Regularly review and update linked media and sources.*

Question: Can I link media and sources to individuals from different branches of my family tree?

Answer: Certainly! Strengthen your family history connections:

1. *Access the profiles of individuals from different branches.*
2. *In the "Gallery" or "Facts" section, choose "Add Media" or "Add a Source."*
3. *Upload relevant media or input source details.*
4. *Save your additions to create a comprehensive family narrative.*

Question: Can I link media and sources to individuals who were part of historical events or lived in significant periods?

Answer: *Absolutely! Showcase their significance:*

1. *Access the profile of the individual.*
2. *Navigate to "Gallery" or "Facts."*
3. *Choose "Add Media" or "Add a Source."*

4. *Upload media or input source details related to their historical role.*
5. *Save your additions to highlight their importance in your family history.*

Question: Can I add family members who have passed away, even if I didn't know them personally?

Answer: *Honor legacy! Include departed family members with respect.*

1. *Open your family tree.*
2. *Click "Add a relative" and select "Deceased."*
3. *Input available details and save.*

Question: How do I begin exploring my ancestral lines on Ancestry.com?

Answer: *Embark on the adventure! Let hints guide you through your roots.*

1. *Select a known ancestor in your tree.*
2. *Click "View Ancestry Hints" to discover potential leads.*
3. *Follow the hints to unveil your lineage.*

Question: What are the essential details I should include when adding an ancestor to my family tree?

> ***Answer:*** *Detail matters! Craft a vivid portrait of your ancestors.*
>
> 1. *Input full name, birth, and death dates.*
> 2. *Include locations and relationships.*

Attach photos and relevant documents

Question: Can I search for historical records related to my family members on Ancestry.com?

> ***Answer:*** *Delve into history! Use Ancestry's vast database to uncover historical records for your family.*
>
> 1. *Utilize Ancestry's search feature.*
> 2. *Find birth certificates, marriage records, etc.*
> 3. *Save records to family members' profiles.*

Question: How can I ensure the accuracy of the information I add to my family tree?

> ***Answer:*** *Precision matters! Build a reliable family narrative.*
>
> 1. *Verify facts using Ancestry's hints.*
> 2. *Cross-reference external sources.*
> 3. *Collaborate with family for validation.*

Question: What should I do if I encounter conflicting information about an ancestor?

> ***Answer:*** *Navigate challenges! Embrace discrepancies as opportunities to learn.*
>
> 1. *Evaluate the reliability of sources.*
> 2. *Document conflicting details in the Notes section.*
> 3. *Seek advice from the Ancestry community.*

Question: How can I extend my ancestral lines beyond the immediate family?

> 1. *Explore hints for siblings and extended family.*
> 2. *Utilize available census records.*

3. *Collaborate with relatives for insightsExpand horizons! Ancestors' stories extend beyond direct lines.*

Question: What do I do if I encounter a gap in my ancestral lines with limited available records?

Answer: *Patience is key! Gaps are opportunities for future discoveries.*

1. *Document the gap in the Notes section.*
2. *Consult Ancestry community forums for advice.*
3. *Explore alternative sources and databases.*

Merging Duplicate Records

Question: How can I merge duplicate records on Ancestry.com?

Answer*: Merging duplicate records on Ancestry.com is a positive step to ensure the accuracy of your family tree. Here's a simple guide to merging duplicates:*

1. ***Navigate to Your Tree:*** *Log in to Ancestry.com and go to your family tree.*

2. ***Identify Duplicates:*** *Look for individuals with potential duplicates. Ancestry may highlight possible duplicates; otherwise, manually review your tree.*
3. ***Access Merge Tool:*** *Click on the person's profile you want to merge. In the top-right corner, click "Tools" and select "Merge with Duplicate."*
4. ***Review Suggestions:*** *Ancestry will suggest potential duplicates. Compare details like names, dates, and locations to ensure accuracy.*
5. ***Select Information:*** *Choose the correct information to retain for each field. Ancestry will prioritize data from both records.*
6. ***Complete Merge:*** *Confirm your choices and finalize the merge. Ancestry.com will consolidate the information into a single, accurate record.*

Merging duplicates streamlines your family tree and enhances the overall research experience.

Question: What should I do if the records contain duplicate parents, spouses, or children during the merge?

Answer: Ensure family accuracy! Navigate duplicate relationships with care during merges.

1. *Prioritize accurate information.*
2. *Merge duplicates carefully.*
3. *Review and update relationships.*

Question: How do I merge duplicate records of the same ancestor in my family tree?

Answer: *Clean up clutter! Ensure accuracy by merging duplicates.*

1. *Identify duplicate profiles.*
2. *Click "Tools" and choose "Merge Duplicate People."*
3. *Follow the prompts to consolidate information.*

Question: What are duplicate records in Family Tree, and why is it essential to merge them?

Answer: *Keep your tree tidy and accurate! Merge duplicate records for a seamless family narrative.*

1. *Identify potential duplicate records.*
2. *Compare details for accuracy.*
3. *Merge duplicates to streamline your tree.*

Question: How can I identify possible duplicate records in Family Tree?

Answer: *Stay organized with ease! Identify potential duplicates using Ancestry's built-in tools.*

1. *Navigate to your Family Tree.*
2. *Look for the "Review Merge" button.*
3. *Utilize Ancestry's hints and alerts.*

Question: What should I do if I am uncertain whether two records are duplicates?

Answer: *Navigate uncertainty with confidence! Trust your instincts and seek support when needed.*

1. *Examine details closely.*
2. *Utilize Ancestry's hints and suggestions.*
3. *Seek advice from community forums.*

Question: How can I merge duplicate records on the Ancestry.com website?

Answer: *Simplify your tree with a few clicks! Merge duplicates effortlessly on the Ancestry website*

1. *Open the Family Tree.*
2. *Locate duplicate individuals.*
3. *Click "Review Merge" and follow prompts.*

Question: How can I merge duplicate records using the Family Tree mobile app?

Answer: *Merge on the go! Keep your tree organized using Ancestry's mobile app.*

1. *Open the Ancestry app.*
2. *Navigate to your Family Tree.*
3. *Tap on a person with potential duplicates.*
4. *Follow app prompts to merge.*

Question: Can I undo a merge if I made a mistake?

Answer: *No worries, mistakes happen! Correct merges easily with Ancestry's "Undo Merge" feature*

1. *Locate the merged person in the Family Tree.*
2. *Click on the person.*
3. *Choose "Tools" and select "Undo Merge."*

Question: What information should I compare before deciding which record to keep in a merge?

Answer: *Choose wisely for accuracy! Compare and prioritize records during the merge process.*

1. *Examine names, dates, and locations.*
2. *Prioritize records with more details.*
3. *Consider source reliability.*

Question: How do I decide which record to keep when merging if there are differences between the records?

Answer: *Make informed decisions! Prioritize accuracy and supporting evidence when deciding on merged records.*

1. *Evaluate the reliability of sources.*
2. *Consider the completeness of details.*
3. *Prioritize records with supporting evidence.*

Question: How can I replace information on the right with information from the left during the merge?

Answer: *Tailor your tree with precision! Use Ancestry's tools to replace information during merges.*

1. *In the merge process, select the information to keep.*
2. *Choose "Replace Right."*
3. *Confirm changes.*

Question: What do I need to do after completing the merge?

Answer: Secure completeness! After merging, review and update details for accuracy.

1. *Review the merged individual's profile.*
2. *Confirm the accuracy of details.*

Update additional information if needed.

Question: Why do merges fail in Family Tree, and how can I avoid merge failures?

Answer: Prevent failures proactively! Verify details and seek community guidance for successful merges.

1. *Check for discrepancies in details.*
2. *Verify sources and information.*
3. *Consult the Ancestry community for advice.*

Question: Can I merge duplicates using Family Tree Lite?

Answer: Merge on the go! Simplify duplicates with Ancestry's Lite app

1. *Open Family Tree Lite.*

2. *Locate duplicates.*
3. *Follow Lite's prompts to merge.*

Question: Where can I find related articles and additional help about merging duplicates in Family Tree?

Answer: Learn continuously! Ancestry's support page is a treasure trove of merging insights.

1. *Visit Ancestry's support page.*
2. *Search for "Merging Duplicates."*
3. *Explore helpful articles and resources.*

Collaborating with Family Members

Question: Why is collaborating with family members essential when building your family tree?

Answer: Celebrate together! Collaboration enhances the family tree-building experience.

1. *Share the joy of discovery.*
2. *Divide tasks for efficiency.*
3. *Gain diverse perspectives.*

Question: How can I collaborate with other family members to fill gaps in my ancestral lines?

Answer: *Together we thrive! A collective effort enhances your family narrative.*

1. *Share your tree with relatives.*
2. *Encourage them to contribute details.*
3. *Regularly communicate and celebrate findings.*

Involving scattered family members is easier than ever with Ancestry.com's collaboration tools. Leverage features like Family Groups and Member Connect to engage relatives across the globe. Schedule virtual meetings, share findings, and make the family history project a global, collective effort.

Question: Can I invite my family members to collaborate on our family tree?

Answer: *Collaboration is key! Invite family members to contribute and enrich the family story together.*

1. *Access your family tree.*
2. *Click "Tree Settings."*

3. *Choose "Invite Family" and enter their email addresses.*

Question: How can I involve family members in the process of building our family tree?

Answer: *Make it a family affair! Engage members with events, tasks, and discoveries.*

1. *Organize a family tree event.*
2. *Assign specific tasks.*
3. *Share interesting findings regularly.*

Question: What are the benefits of creating a private family group on Ancestry.com for collaboration?

Answer*: Ensure privacy! Use private groups for secure and focused collaboration.*

1. *Create a private group.*
2. *Invite family members.*
3. *Share and collaborate securely.*

Question: How can I encourage family members to participate actively in the family tree-building process?

Answer: Infuse enthusiasm! Emphasize the significance and joy of participation.

1. *Highlight the importance.*
2. *Showcase the fun aspects.*
3. *Acknowledge and celebrate contributions.*

Question: *What are some effective ways to divide research tasks among family members to maximize efficiency?*

Answer: Optimize efforts! Tailor tasks based on strengths for efficient collaboration.

1. *Identify individual strengths.*
2. *Assign specific branches or time periods.*
3. *Schedule regular check-ins.*

Question: How can we verify the accuracy of information shared by different family members during collaboration?

Answer: Ensure accuracy! Foster open communication and implement fact-checking.

1. *Cross-verify with reliable sources.*
2. *Discuss discrepancies openly.*
3. *Establish a fact-checking system.*

Question: Are there any tools or features on Ancestry.com that facilitate collaboration among family members?

Answer: To enhance collaboration among family members on Ancestry.com, leverage the following tools and features:

1. ***Utilize Tree Collaboration Tools:***
   - *Access Ancestry's Tree Collaboration Tools to work collaboratively on family trees.*
   - *Share your family tree with specific family members, allowing them to contribute and edit.*

- *Ensure that your tree is set to "Private" or "Public with Edit Access" to enable collaboration.*

2. ***Assign Tasks and Review Changes:***
    - *Within your family tree, assign tasks to different family members based on their expertise or interest.*
    - *Regularly review and track changes made by collaborators. Ancestry keeps a log of modifications for transparency.*
3. ***Explore the Ancestry Community:***
    - *Engage with the Ancestry community through the Community tab on the homepage.*
    - *Participate in discussion boards, connect with other researchers, and share your discoveries.*
    - *Ancestry's community provides a platform for exchanging knowledge, seeking advice, and collaborating with a wider genealogy audience.*
4. ***Connect & Collaborate Feature**:*
    - *Utilize Ancestry's "Connect & Collaborate" feature, which facilitates*

communication and sharing among family members.

- *This feature is designed to help you discover a fuller family story by connecting and collaborating with relatives.*

5. ***Check for Collaboration Tools Updates:***
    - *Keep an eye on updates and new collaboration tools that Ancestry may introduce to enhance the collaborative experience.*

Question: How can we handle disagreements or conflicting information among family members during collaboration?

1. *Encourage open dialogue.*
2. *Seek a consensus.*
3. *Document alternative perspectives.*

Question: What role does storytelling play in collaborating with family members?

Answer: *Bring stories to life! Integrate personal narratives for a richer family tree.*

1. *Share personal anecdotes.*

2. *Incorporate oral histories.*
3. *Weave narratives into the tree.*

Question: How can we encourage older family members to share their oral history and experiences?

> ***Answer:*** *Honor experiences! Make sharing comfortable and enjoyable for older family members.*
>
> 1. *Conduct dedicated interviews.*
> 2. *Create a comfortable environment.*
> 3. *Use multimedia for recording.*

Question: What steps can we take to preserve family traditions and cultural practices during collaboration?

> ***Answer:*** *Celebrate heritage! Preserve traditions in a dedicated section for future generations.*
>
> 1. *Document traditions meticulously.*
> 2. *Create a separate section for cultural practices.*
> 3. *Encourage discussions and additions.*

Question: How can we ensure that all family members have equal access to the collaborative efforts and information on Ancestry.com?

Answer: Promote equality! Establish clear access rules and provide training for all members.

1. *Set clear access permissions.*
2. *Conduct training sessions.*
3. *Foster an inclusive atmosphere.*

Question: What are some creative ways to engage younger family members in the family tree-building process?

Answer: Make the family tree-building process enjoyable for younger members by incorporating interactive and creative elements:

1. ***Use Interactive Platforms:***

   Opt for online platforms or apps designed for interactive family tree creation.

Explore tools that allow collaborative input and engagement from multiple family members.

2. ***Gamify the Research Process:***

   Turn the family tree-building into a game by creating challenges or quests.

   Introduce rewards or achievements for reaching milestones or discovering new family connections.

   Incorporate friendly competition among younger family members to make the process exciting.

3. ***Incorporate Multimedia Elements:***

   Add a visual and storytelling aspect by including photos, videos, and audio clips of family members.

   Encourage younger members to interview older relatives and record their stories.

   Create a multimedia-rich family tree that visually represents the family's history and traditions.

4. ***Family Tree Art and Crafts:***

Combine creativity with genealogy by organizing art and craft sessions.

Design family tree posters or 3D structures, allowing younger members to express their artistic side while learning about their heritage.

5. ***Storytelling Sessions:***

   Host storytelling sessions where older family members share anecdotes and stories related to the family's history.

   Encourage younger members to illustrate these stories, creating a blend of oral history and visual representation.

6. ***Virtual Family Reunions:***

   Plan virtual family reunions where family members can share and discuss their progress in building the family tree.

Foster a sense of connection and collaboration, making the family tree-building process a shared experience.

Question: What guidelines should we establish to maintain data privacy and security while collaborating online?

> ***Answer:*** *Prioritize security! Educate and use secure tools for a protected collaborative environment.*
>
> 1. *Educate members on privacy.*
> 2. *Use private collaboration tools.*
> 3. *Regularly update security measures.*

Question: How can we celebrate milestones and achievements in the collaborative journey of building our family tree?

> ***Answer****: Celebrate success! Recognize milestones and contributions for a rewarding journey.*
>
> 1. *Establish milestone markers.*
> 2. *Acknowledge individual contributions.*
> 3. *Host virtual celebrations.*

Additional Resources:

1. *Ancestry.com - Managing Sources in Trees*
2. *Ancestry.com - Uploading Media*

3. *Ancestry.com - Attaching a Source to Multiple People*
4. *YouTube - Using Media in Your Ancestry Family Tree*
5. *Ancestry.com - Adding People to a Tree*
6. *YouTube - DO THIS To Link Photos to Events in Your Ancestry Family Tree*
7. *Adding People to a Tree - Ancestry® Support*
8. *Getting Started, Lesson 4: Collaboration*
9. *Change person in Family Tree from living to dead*
10. *Getting Started, Lesson 2: Building Your Tree*
11. *Requesting Access to the Account of an Ancestry®...*
12. *Creating A Family Tree On Ancestry - YouTube*
13. *How does AncestryDNA® work?*
14. *Why Use Ancestry®?*
15. *Ancestry.com: Tips and Tricks for Beginners*
16. *AncestryDNA® Test Accuracy and Precision*
17. *What are the benefits of using Ancestry.com over doing family tree research at a library*
18. *Ancestry Support - Merging Duplicate People*
19. *Ancestry Support - Family Groups*
20. *Senior Living Activity - 8 Ways to Preserve Your Family History*

21. *YouTube - Fixing Duplicates in Ancestry.com Family Trees*
22. *Ancestry Support - Collaboration Lesson*
23. *Ancestry Support - Merging Duplicate People in the Ancestry App*

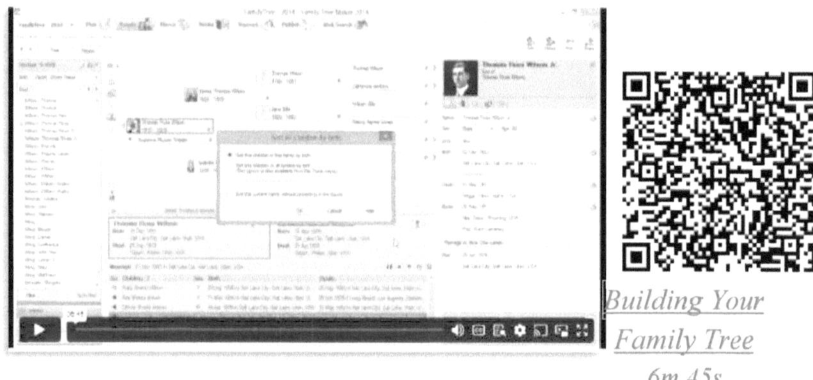

Building Your Family Tree 6m 45s

Chapter 4
Searching and Accessing Records

How to Conduct Effective Searches

Question: How can I ensure my research is accurate and well-documented?

Answer: *When researching on Ancestry.com, it's crucial to follow best practices for accuracy and documentation:*

Cite your sources: *Always record the source information for each document you find, including the website address, archive name, and record details. This will allow you to easily locate the information again and verify its authenticity.*

Evaluate the evidence: *Don't take information at face value. Analyze each document critically, considering its context, potential biases.*

Question: What strategies can I use to break through brick walls with difficult ancestors?

Answer: *Break through brick walls systematically:*

- ***Reevaluate existing data:*** *Confirm accuracy and explore alternative interpretations.*
- ***Expand search parameters****: Utilize wildcard characters, consider phonetic variations, and broaden geographical scopes.*
- ***Explore diverse record collections:*** *Investigate newspapers, military records, and local archives beyond standard census and vital records.*
- ***Network and seek advice:*** *Engage with the genealogy community for fresh perspectives and strategies.*
- ***Utilize the Ancestry.com Wiki and Learning Center:*** *Access resources for expert guidance on overcoming specific challenges.*

Question: How do I access census data and vital records on Ancestry.com for my ancestors?

Answer:

1. *Navigate to Ancestry.com and log in to your account.*
2. *Use the search bar to enter your ancestor's name, along with additional details like birth year and location.*
3. *Explore the search results, focusing on census records and vital records.*
4. *Click on relevant records to view detailed information about your ancestor.*
5. *Save and attach records to your ancestor's profile for future reference.*

Question: How can I make the most of census data for my genealogy research?

Answer: *Maximize census data:*

- ***Extract family structures:*** *Identify household members and relationships.*

- ***Note occupations and residences:*** *Uncover socioeconomic details and migration patterns.*
- ***Utilize birthplaces and ages:*** *Refine search parameters and cross-reference with other records.*
- ***Explore neighbors:*** *Investigate neighboring households for potential familial connections.*
- ***Combine with vital records:*** *Use census details to supplement birth, marriage, and death records.*

Question: Can I access census data and vital records from different countries on Ancestry.com?

Answer: *Yes, Ancestry.com provides access to international records. Use the search filters to specify the country of interest and explore relevant collections for census data and vital records.*

Question: How can I verify the accuracy of vital records found on Ancestry.com?

Answer: *Verify vital records:*

- ***Cross-reference with multiple sources:*** *Confirm information using other records.*
- ***Check for consistency:*** *Ensure details align with known facts and family narratives.*
- ***Review original documents:*** *If available, inspect the actual records for accuracy.*
- ***Explore alternative records:*** *Seek supporting evidence from diverse sources*

Question: What resources can I use on Ancestry.com to learn more about genealogy research?

Answer: *Ancestry.com offers a wealth of resources to help you learn genealogy research skills:*

Learning Center: *Access articles, webinars, podcasts, and videos covering various genealogy topics, from beginner basics to advanced research techniques.*

Genealogy Glossary: *Learn the definitions of common genealogy terms and abbreviations to navigate the research process effectively.*

Research Guides: *Find guides focused on specific research areas, such as African*

American genealogy, immigration records, or military records. These guides offer tailored advice and resources for efficient research in those areas.

Blog: *Stay up-to-date on the latest genealogy news, trends, and tips through the Ancestry blog.*

Expert Q&A: *Get your research questions answered by experienced genealogists during scheduled Q&A sessions.*

Question: What strategies can I use to research ancestors from different countries or cultures?

Answer: *Diversity enriches! Immerse yourself in global ancestry exploration.*

1. *Utilize Ancestry's global search feature.*
2. *Explore country-specific databases.*
3. *Connect with Ancestry community members from those regions.*

Question: What are some general tips for conducting effective searches on Ancestry.com?

Answer: *Start with specific details like names, dates, and locations. Refine your search with filters and explore related records for comprehensive results.*

Question: What strategies can I employ to overcome common challenges in finding ancestors with common names?

Answer: *Focus on additional details like birthdates, locations, and family members. Use filters wisely and explore alternative records beyond the obvious.*

Question: What should I do if my initial search does not yield any relevant results?

Answer: *Refine your search criteria by being less specific or removing filters. Experiment with variations and explore different record collections for better outcomes.*

Question: How can I make the most of the search suggestions and related records feature on Ancestry.com?

Answer: *Embrace suggestions to discover new leads. Explore related records for a comprehensive view of your ancestors' lives, uncovering hidden gems.*

Question: How can I conduct searches in specific record collections or databases on Ancestry.com?

Answer: *Navigate to "Search" and choose "Card Catalog." Explore specific databases by filtering collections based on location, date, or type for targeted searches.*

Question: What is the best approach to searching for ancestors with common name variations due to cultural or linguistic differences?

Answer: *Expand your search by considering cultural variations. Utilize wildcards and explore alternative spellings to capture diverse records within the desired cultural context.*

Question: How can I effectively search for female ancestors whose names might have changed due to marriage?

Answer: *Search using maiden and married names. Utilize filters for gender, spouses, and explore marriage records to trace the evolution of female ancestors' names.*

Question: What strategies can I use to search for ancestors with limited information, such as missing birth dates or locations?

Answer: *Start broad, focusing on known details. Gradually narrow down using filters and explore records related to family members for clues on missing information.*

Question: What can I do if I encounter language barriers while searching for records in foreign countries?

Answer: *Collaborate with local researchers or use translation tools. Explore international genealogy forums for assistance. Language* *barriers can be overcome through community support.*

Question: How can I verify the authenticity and accuracy of records found during my searches?

Answer: *Cross-reference records with multiple sources. Validate information using primary sources and consider the credibility of the record provider for accuracy.*

Question: What resources and reference materials can I consult to improve my search skills and techniques?

Answer: *Explore Ancestry's learning resources, including tutorials, articles, and forums. Utilize external guides and books on genealogy for a holistic understanding.*

Question: How can I overcome challenges and roadblocks in my research?

Answer: *It's natural to encounter challenges during your research journey. Here are some tips to overcome them:*

Consult the Ancestry.com Help Center: *Access a searchable database of articles and FAQs covering common research challenges and solutions.*

Join online communities: *Connect with other researchers facing similar challenges. Share your experiences, ask for advice, and learn from others' successes and struggles.*

Contact Ancestry.com support: If *you need further assistance, contact Ancestry.com's customer support team who can provide personalized guidance and troubleshoot your research issues.*

Take breaks and come back later: *Don't get discouraged by roadblocks. Taking breaks and revisiting your research with fresh eyes can often lead to breakthroughs.*

Seek professional help: Consider *hiring a professional genealogist if you encounter complex challenges or need assistance with specialized research areas.*

Question: How can I use the date range filter to narrow down search results to a specific time period?

> ***Answer:*** *Apply the date range filter to focus on a specific time frame. Specify birth, marriage, or death years to tailor your search results effectively.*

Question: How can I effectively use the record type filter to search for specific types of records, like census or immigration records?

> ***Answer:*** *Apply the record type filter to refine your search. Choose categories such as census or immigration to focus on specific record types relevant to your genealogical goals.*

Question: What is the benefit of using the collection filter, and how can it help me search within specific record collections?

> ***Answer:*** *The collection filter allows you to target specific databases. Use it to explore*

unique record collections relevant to your ancestors, enhancing the precision of your searches.

Question: What is the purpose of the place filter, and how can it help in finding records about my ancestors in a particular location?

Answer: *Utilize the place filter to narrow down searches to specific locations. This helps you explore records relevant to your ancestors in their specific geographical context.*

Question: How can I use the "Any Event" filter to broaden my search and explore records that may not have specific event dates or locations?

Answer: *Apply the "Any Event" filter to cast a wider net. This helps uncover records where specific dates or locations might be unclear, providing a broader view of your ancestors' lives.*

Question: What are some advanced search options, and how can I use them to refine my search further?

Answer: *Ancestry.com offers advanced search options for precise results. Use filters like date range, location, and record type. Leverage the "Exact" search for pinpoint accuracy. Experiment with combinations to tailor searches to your*

Question: How can I utilize wildcards and fuzzy search to find records with similar spellings or variations of names?

Answer: *Use wildcards (*) to replace unknown letters and fuzzy search in the name field for variations. Experiment with different spellings to capture diverse records.*

Question: How can I use search operators (e.g., AND, OR, NOT) to create more complex and targeted searches?

Answer: *Combine operators for precision. Use AND to narrow, OR for alternatives, and NOT* *to exclude. Craft complex queries like "John AND (Smith OR Johnson)" for tailored results.*

Question: What are some best practices for using search operators like AND, OR, and NOT?

Answer: *Combine search operators for precision. Use AND to narrow results, OR for alternatives, and NOT to exclude terms. Experiment to refine your search effectively.*

Question: How can I use the Soundex feature to find records with similar-sounding names?

Answer: *To find records with similar-sounding names using Soundex on Ancestry:*

Activate Soundex Option:

While conducting a search, look for the Soundex option.

Enable it to include names with phonetic similarities in the search results.

Search with Phonetic Variations:

The Soundex algorithm considers names that sound alike but may have different spellings.

This widens the search scope, helping you discover records with potential spelling variations.

Explore Phonetic Matches:

Results obtained with Soundex may include names pronounced similarly to the one you entered.

Explore these matches to identify variations in spelling that conventional searches might miss.

Utilize Spelling Variations:

Combine Soundex with spelling variations for a comprehensive search.

Ancestry's Soundex feature is designed to display results for names with similar pronunciations, enhancing the chances of finding relevant records.

Refine Search Results:

Review the search results carefully, considering both exact matches and those with similar sounds.

Use additional filters and information to refine your search further.

Question: What is Soundex, and how can I utilize it to find records with similar-sounding names?

Answer: *Soundex groups with similar-sounding names. Enable Soundex in your search for phonetic matches. This broadens your results, helping uncover records with names that sound alike.*

Question: How can I efficiently use the "Exact" search option to find records with names that match exactly?

Answer: *Choose the "Exact" search to find names precisely. Ideal for unique names, this ensures accurate matches. Combine with other filters for a comprehensive search.*

Question: How do I use the "Keyword" search option to explore records based on specific keywords or phrases?

Answer: *Utilize "Keyword" for focused searches. Enter specific terms like occupations or locations. Experiment with different keywords to uncover diverse records.*

Question: Can I combine filters and advanced search options to conduct highly targeted searches?

Answer: *Absolutely! Combine filters for refined searches. For instance, combine a date range, location, and record type to hone in on specific ancestors. Experiment for optimal results.*

Question: What strategies can I employ to adjust filters and search options if my initial search does not yield relevant results?

Answer: *If initial results are sparse, broaden filters or remove them. Adjust date ranges and use wildcards. Explore different record collections for potential matches.*

Question: How can I save and reuse search filters for future searches?

Answer: *After setting filters, click "Save Search." This preserves your criteria for future use. Access saved searches from your profile for convenient reuse.*

Question: Are there additional resources or tutorials available on Ancestry.com to improve my skills in utilizing filters and advanced search options effectively?

Answer: *Absolutely! Ancestry.com offers valuable resources to boost your skills in utilizing filters and advanced search options effectively:*

Getting Started Lessons:

- *Explore the "Getting Started" section on Ancestry.com.*
- *Engage with interactive lessons tailored for users at various skill levels.*

Support Center Articles:

- *Visit the Ancestry Support Center for comprehensive articles.*
- *Find detailed tutorials on leveraging filters and advanced search options.*

Search Tips and Tricks:

- *Ancestry Anne's Top 10 Search Tips provide practical insights.*

- *Access Anne's tips, including advanced search techniques, to refine your strategies.*

Advanced Filters in Ancestry Pro Tools:

- *Utilize advanced filters available in Ancestry Pro Tools.*
- *These filters help in searching, grouping, and sorting individuals based on key details beyond names.*

Online Communities and Forums:

- *Join Ancestry.com online communities and forums.*
- *Engage with experienced users to exchange tips and tricks for effective searching.*

Accessing Historical Records, Census Data, and Vital Records

Question: How can I access historical records that are not yet digitized on Ancestry.com?

Answer: *Contact local archives or visit in person. Explore offline resources like libraries* *and historical societies. Expand your research beyond digital records.*

Question: How do I find and add historical records from external sources to my immediate family members' profiles?

Answer: *Expand horizons! Validate family history with external sources.*

1. *Open a family member's profile.*
2. *Click "Facts" and choose "Add a fact."*
3. *Select "Source" and input external records.*

Question: How can I access historical birth records on Ancestry.com?

Answer: *It's not that hard. Just follow these steps:*

Navigate to the "Search" tab,

Select "Birth, Marriage & Death," and enter known details.

Refine with filters and explore various collections for comprehensive birth records.

Question: How can I use vital records to trace my ancestor's life events and milestones?

Answer: *Vital records serve as key milestones in your ancestor's life. Use them to:*

1. *Determine birthdates and birthplaces.*
2. *Track marriages and spouses.*
3. *Uncover death details, including burial locations.*
4. *Establish a chronological timeline of your ancestor's life.*

Question: What types of vital records are available on Ancestry.com, and how can they assist my research?

Answer: *Ancestry.com offers various vital records such as birth, marriage, and death certificates. These records are crucial for:*

1. *Confirming life events and dates.*
2. *Establishing familial connections.*
3. *Uncovering critical details for comprehensive family histories.*

Question: How can I access and view the full details of census records and vital records on Ancestry.com?

Answer: *To access full details on Ancestry.com:*

1. *Subscribe to a paid plan for comprehensive access.*
2. *Click on individual records in your search results.*
3. *Evaluate record details such as names, dates, and locations.*
4. *Utilize advanced search features for targeted results.*

Question: Can I download or save census data and vital records from Ancestry.com?

Answer: *Yes, you can save census data and vital records on Ancestry.com:*

1. *Open the desired record.*
2. *Look for a "Save" or "Download" option.*
3. *Follow the prompts to store records for offline use.*

Question: Can I access birth, marriage, and death records for free on Ancestry.com?

Answer: *While some records are available for free, a subscription is typically required for full access to birth, marriage, and death records on Ancestry.com. Explore the platform's free trial or consider accessing records through local archives and libraries.*

Question: What is census data, and how can they help with my genealogy research?

Answer: *Census data provides a snapshot of individuals and households at specific times. Utilize census records on Ancestry.com to:*

1. *Trace family migrations.*
2. *Identify relationships and family structures.*
3. *Discover occupation and economic status.*
4. *Uncover vital information for further research.*

Question: How do I interpret the information in census data and vital records for my research?

Answer: *Interpret census data and vital records effectively:*

- ***Understand column headings:*** *Grasp the meaning of each column in census records.*
- ***Extract key details:*** *Focus on names, ages, relationships, occupations, and residences.*
- ***Consider cultural context:*** *Be aware of naming conventions and family structures of the time.*
- *Note discrepancies: Record inconsistencies for further investigation.*
- *Cross-reference with other records: Compare census data with vital records for comprehensive insights.*

Question: Can I download or save census data and vital records from Ancestry.com?

> ***Answer:*** *Ancestry.com allows users to download and save records. Locate the record of interest and look for a download or save option. This feature facilitates offline access and preserves records for future reference.*

Question: How can I use census data to learn more about my ancestor's living conditions and family structure?

Answer: *Dive deep into census data:*

- ***Explore occupation details:*** *Uncover livelihoods and economic status.*
- ***Identify household members:*** *Understand family structures and relationships.*
- ***Note property ownership:*** *Discover the economic standing and stability.*
- ***Examine education levels:*** *Gain insights into the family's intellectual background.*

Question: How can I use vital records to trace my ancestor's life events and milestones?

Answer: *Leverage vital records:*

- ***Birth records:*** *Reveal birth dates, locations, and parentage.*
- ***Marriage records:*** *Provide marriage dates, spouses, and sometimes parents.*
- ***Death records:*** *Offer death dates, locations, and sometimes cause of death.*

- ***Compile a timeline:*** *Sequence events to trace your ancestor's life journey.*

Question: How do I find and access specific types of vital records, such as marriage certificates or death records?

Answer:

1. *On Ancestry.com, use the search bar and enter your ancestor's details.*
2. *Filter results by selecting "Birth, Marriage, Death."*
3. *Further narrow down by choosing the specific record type like "Marriage" or "Death."*
4. *Browse the relevant search results and click on individual records for more information.*

Question: How do I access historical marriage records to learn about my ancestors' marital unions?

Answer: *Choose "Marriage" under "Birth, Marriage & Death" in the "Search" tab. Input details and apply filters for tailored results, unraveling your ancestors' marital stories.*

Question: Can I access historical death records to find information about my deceased ancestors?

Answer: *Absolutely! To access historical death records and unveil details about your deceased ancestors on Ancestry:*

1. *Navigate to the Vital Records category.*
2. *Select "Death" under "Birth, Marriage & Death."*
3. *Input specific details about your ancestor.*
4. *Utilize filters for more precise search results.*
5. *Explore available collections like Death Certificates and specific state indexes.*
6. *Uncover the rich stories hidden in your ancestors' death records.*

Question: How can I access census data from different time periods on Ancestry.com?

Answer: *Visit the "Census & Voter Lists" section. Choose the desired year and location. Input ancestor details, apply filters, and dive into the rich details of their lives.*

Question: What types of information can I find in census records on Ancestry.com?

Answer: *Census records provide a snapshot of your ancestors' lives. Discover details like names, ages, occupations, and family relationships. Use filters to extract specific insights.*

Question: How do I access census data from specific countries on Ancestry.com?

Answer: *Ancestry.com provides a vast collection of international census data. To access census records from a specific country, follow these steps:*

- *Begin by navigating to the "Search" tab.*
- *Select "Card Catalog" and filter by location.*
- *Choosing the desired country.*
- *Explore available census collections for comprehensive insights into your ancestors' lives.*
- *Utilize search filters to narrow results based on names, dates, and other details.*

Question: Can I access census records from different U.S. states on Ancestry.com?

Answer: *Absolutely! Ancestry.com boasts an extensive U.S. Federal Census Collection. To access state-specific records, visit the "Search" tab, choose "Card Catalog," and filter by the desired state.*

Explore census records rich with details about your ancestors' residences, ages, and more. Use search options to refine your quest and uncover valuable information.

Question: How can I access historical immigration records to learn about my ancestors' arrival in a new country?

Answer: *Delve into your ancestors' immigration stories on Ancestry.com. Navigate to the "Search" tab, select "Immigration & Emigration," and enter relevant details. Explore passenger lists, border crossings, and other records documenting their journey. Use search filters to enhance accuracy and piece together the narrative of your ancestors' arrival.*

Question: Can I access ship passenger lists on Ancestry.com for my ancestors who immigrated to the United States?

> ***Answer:*** *Absolutely! To find ship passenger lists, visit the "Search" tab, select "Immigration & Emigration," and enter ancestor details. Explore the "U.S. Immigration Collection" for comprehensive ship manifests. Utilize filters to refine searches, making it easier to trace your ancestors' voyage to the United States.*

Question: How do I access historical military records to find information about my ancestors' military service?

> ***Answer:*** *Discover your ancestors' military journeys with Ancestry.com's extensive military records. Visit the "Search" tab, select "Military," and enter details. Uncover service records, enlistment documents, and more. Leverage filters for precision, unveiling a detailed account of your ancestors' military service.*

Question: Can I access pension records on Ancestry.com to learn about my ancestors' military benefits?

> ***Answer:*** *Absolutely! Ancestry.com houses a wealth of pension records. To access them, visit the "Search" tab, choose "Military," and input ancestor details. Explore pension files for insights into military benefits and the lives of your ancestors post-service. Refine searches using filters for accurate and detailed results.*

Question: How can I access historical naturalization records to find information about my ancestors' path to citizenship?

> ***Answer:*** *Trace your ancestors' path to citizenship on Ancestry.com by visiting the "Search" tab and selecting "Immigration & Emigration." Enter details to explore naturalization records. Uncover valuable information about their journey to becoming citizens and utilize search filters for precise results.*

Question: Can I access historical land and property records to trace my ancestors' land ownership and transactions?

> ***Answer:*** *Absolutely! Ancestry.com offers an extensive collection of land and property records. Navigate to the "Search" tab, choose "Card Catalog," and select "Land Records." Enter ancestor details to uncover deeds, land grants, and transactions. Use filters to refine searches, piecing together the story of your ancestors' land ownership.*

Question: How do I access church records on Ancestry.com to find information about baptisms, marriages, and burials?

> ***Answer:*** *Embark on a journey through your ancestors' spiritual milestones on Ancestry.com. Visit the "Search" tab, select "Card Catalog," and choose "Church Records." Enter details to explore baptisms, marriages, and burials. Utilize filters for accurate and meaningful discoveries about your ancestors' spiritual heritage.*

Additional Resources:

1. *Search Tips - Ancestry.com*
2. *Overcoming Roadblocks in Your Research - Ancestry® Support*
3. *Getting Started, Lesson 5: Search Tips*
4. *Spelling Doesn't Count: Tips for Finding Your Ancestors*
5. *Getting Started, Lesson 5: Search Tips*
6. *Searching with Wild Cards - Ancestry® Support*
7. *Searching with Soundex - Ancestry® Support*
8. *Search Tips - Ancestry.com*
9. *Searching with Spelling Variations - Ancestry® Support*

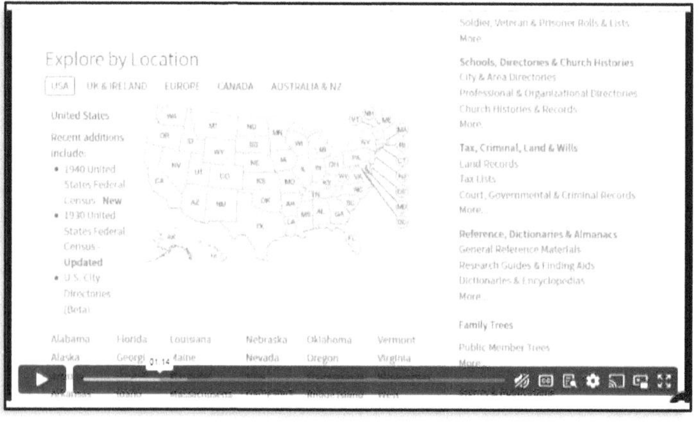

What Records Are Out There?

- Vital Records - Civil & Church
- Census
- Parish Records
- Wills
- Cemetery/MI's
- Land
- Newspapers
- Directories
- Passenger Lists
- Military
- Genealogies
- History
- Apprenticeship
- Biographies
- Poor Law
- Home Children
- School
- Court

Chapter 5
Uploading and Managing Documents Photos Etc…

Preserving Family Photos and Documents

Question: How can I preserve and share family photos and documents on Ancestry.com?

Answer: *Safeguard your family's legacy by preserving and sharing photos on Ancestry.com. Create a family tree, attach photos, and add relevant documents. Encourage collaboration by inviting family members to contribute. Share your discoveries, fostering a sense of connection and preserving your family's history for future generations.*

Question: Can I upload media for multiple family members at once?

Answer: *Yes, you can efficiently upload media for multiple family members on Ancestry.com.*

1. *Begin by navigating to the "Family Tree" tab.*
2. *Selecting the desired person.*
3. *Click on the "Media" tab within their profile.*
4. *Here, you can upload photos, documents, and more by selecting "Add Media."*

Ensure your family's history is richly documented by seamlessly associating media with various family members in a single upload session.

Question: How can I link a specific photo or document to a particular individual in my family tree?

Answer: *Linking photos or documents to specific individuals is a breeze on Ancestry.com.*

From the person's profile page,

Click on "Profile," then select "Add Media."

Choose the relevant photo or document and link it to the individual by selecting their name from the dropdown menu.

This ensures that your family tree becomes a visually engaging and comprehensive repository of your ancestors' stories.

Question: Are there any restrictions on the file types I can upload?

Answer: *Ancestry.com supports various file types for media uploads, ensuring flexibility and accessibility. You can upload common image formats, such as JPEG and PNG, as well as document formats like PDF. Before uploading, verify that the file size is 15 MB or smaller to ensure a smooth and efficient process.*

Question: How can I ensure the photos/documents I upload are preserved for the long term?

Answer: *Rest assured, Ancestry.com is committed to preserving your uploaded photos and documents for the long term. The platform employs robust archival practices to safeguard your family history. Regularly back up your data, and consider downloading your tree* *periodically to ensure an additional layer of protection.*

Question: Is there a limit to the number of photos/documents I can upload?

Answer: *There's no need to limit your storytelling! Ancestry.com provides ample space for your family's journey. You can upload a substantial number of photos and documents to create a comprehensive narrative of your family history.*

Feel free to enrich your tree with visual elements that capture the essence of your ancestors' lives.

Question: Can I add descriptions or captions to the photos/documents I upload?

Answer: *Absolutely! Enhance the storytelling of your family history by adding descriptions or captions to the photos and documents you upload on Ancestry.com.*

Provide context, share anecdotes, and create a more vivid picture of your ancestors' lives.

Simply edit the media details to include meaningful descriptions that contribute to the richness of your family tree.

Question: Can I share the photos/documents I upload with other family members?

Answer: *Sharing your family history is a delightful experience on Ancestry.com. Easily share photos and documents with other family members by inviting them to your tree. Collaborate on building a collective narrative, fostering a sense of connection and shared heritage.*

Question: Is there a way to organize my uploaded photos/documents?

Answer: *Ancestry.com allows you to maintain order in your family history archive. Organize your uploaded photos and documents by creating albums. Group related media together to tell cohesive stories, making it easier to navigate and explore your family's rich heritage.*

Question: How can I add photos/documents to an existing album?

Answer: *To add photos or documents to an existing album on Ancestry.com,*

Go to the "Family Tree" tab and select "Media."

Click on the desired album,

then choose "Add Media."

Select the photos or documents you want to include, ensuring your family history albums continue to grow and tell a more complete story.

Question: Can I create separate albums for different branches of my family?

Answer: *Absolutely! Organize your family history creatively by creating separate albums for different branches of your family on Ancestry.com. From the "Family Tree" tab, navigate to "Media," select "Create a New Album," and customize it to represent distinct branches. This adds a visual dimension to your family history, making it more accessible and engaging.*

Question: Can I upload photos/documents that are physically stored in an album or binder?

> ***Answer:*** *Yes, you can seamlessly digitize and upload photos or documents that are physically stored in albums or binders to Ancestry.com.*
>
> *Leverage the platform's upload functionality by selecting the relevant individual's profile, clicking on "Add Media," and choosing the desired files. Preserve and share your family's treasured memories with ease.*

Question: How can I view and manage the photos/documents I've uploaded on Ancestry.com?

> ***Answer:*** *Managing your uploaded photos and documents is effortless on Ancestry.com.*
>
> *Simply go to the "Family Tree" tab,*
>
> *Select "Media,"*
>
> *You'll find a comprehensive view of all your uploaded items.*

From here, you can easily edit details, move media between albums, and ensure your family history remains organized and accessible.

Question: Can I add photos/documents to my family tree directly from the Ancestry.com mobile app?

Answer: *Absolutely! Enriching your family tree with photos and documents is a mobile-friendly experience on Ancestry.com. Utilize the mobile app by selecting the individual's profile, tapping on "Add Media," and seamlessly uploading photos or documents directly from your mobile device. Share your family's story on the go!*

Question: Are there any privacy settings for the photos/documents I upload?

Answer: *Ancestry.com prioritizes your privacy. You can control who sees the photos and documents you upload by adjusting privacy settings. When uploading, choose the desired privacy level—whether for public view, restricted to your tree, or accessible only to* *specific individuals. This ensures a tailored and secure sharing experience.*

Question: How can I include family photos and documents for each family member?

Answer: *Make your family tree vibrant! Adding photos and documents brings your ancestors to life. Share their stories visually.*

1. ***Open a Family Member's Profile:***
   - *Log in to your Ancestry account.*
   - *Navigate to the family tree and select the specific family member you want to enhance with photos and documents.*
2. ***Access the Gallery Section:***
   - *Within the family member's profile, locate and click on the "Gallery" section*
   - *This is where you can manage, and view media associated with the selected individual.*
4. ***Upload Photos and Documents:***
   - *In the Gallery section, look for options like "Add Media" or "Upload."*
   - *Click on the appropriate button to initiate the media upload process.*

5. ***Select Media Type:***

- *Choose whether you want to add photos, documents, or other media types.*
- *For photos, select the image file from your device.*
- *For documents, you can upload scanned records or other relevant files.*

6. ***Provide Context and Details:***

- *Add titles, descriptions, and dates to the uploaded media to provide context and organize information.*
    - *This step is crucial for creating a comprehensive visual narrative of your family history.*

7. ***Save Changes:***

- *Once you've uploaded the photos or documents and added relevant details, don't forget to save your changes.*

8. ***Repeat for Each Family Member:***

- *Repeat these steps for every family member you wish to enhance with visual elements.*
- *Each family member's profile can have its own unique set of photos and documents.*

Upload photos, documents, and stories

Question: How can I ensure the preservation of family heirlooms and documents?

Answer: *To ensure the preservation of family heirlooms and documents, follow expert advice from sources like Legacy Tree. Implement proper storage techniques, use acid-free materials, and consider professional preservation services for delicate items. This guarantees your treasures remain intact for future generations.*

Uploading Media to Ancestry.com

Question: How do I upload photos and documents to Ancestry.com?

Answer: *Uploading is a breeze! Visit the person's profile, click "Gallery," then "Add a Photo" or "Add a Document." Choose the file from your computer, add a title, and click "Save." Your family history will shine with these visual treasures.*

Question: Can I upload photos and documents related to census records on Ancestry.com?

> ***Answer:*** *Absolutely! Enhance your ancestors' profiles by attaching photos or documents related to census records. In the individual's profile, go to "Gallery" and click "Add a Photo" or "Add a Document." Connect these visuals to provide a comprehensive family history.*

Question: How do I upload census data to Ancestry.com?

> ***Answer:*** *While you can't upload raw census data, you can document census details manually. Visit the person's profile, click "Facts and Sources," then "Add a Fact" to include census information. Attach related photos or documents for a complete family history picture.*

Question: Can I upload vital records such as birth certificates and death certificates to Ancestry.com?

Answer: *Absolutely! Strengthen your family history with vital records. In the individual's profile, go to "Gallery" and click "Add a Document." Upload birth certificates, death certificates, or any essential records to provide a comprehensive view of your ancestors' lives.*

Question: How do I attach vital records to individuals in my family tree on Ancestry.com?

Answer: *Attaching vital records is simple.*

In the individual's profile,

- *go to "Gallery" and click "Add a Document."*
- *Choose the vital record file,*
- *add a title,*
- *save.*

This creates a valuable link between the document and your ancestor's profile.

Question: Is there a limit to the number of photos and documents I can upload on Ancestry.com?

Answer: *Ancestry.com offers generous storage. While there's no set limit, be mindful of image size and quality. Optimize files for efficient storage and ensure your family history remains visually captivating.*

Question: Can I upload photos and documents from my mobile device to Ancestry.com?

Answer: *Absolutely! Enrich your family history on the go. Use the Ancestry.com mobile app, navigate to the individual's profile, click "Gallery," and choose "Add a Photo" or "Add a Document." Capture and share family memories directly from your mobile device.*

Question: Can I upload scanned images of historical photos to Ancestry.com?

Answer: *Certainly! Preserve historical photos by scanning them into digital files. In the individual's profile, click "Gallery," then "Add a Photo." Select the scanned image, add* *details, and save. Your ancestors' visuals will be safeguarded and accessible for generations.*

Question: Can I upload documents written in languages other than English to Ancestry.com?

Answer: *Absolutely! Celebrate your diverse heritage by uploading documents in any language. In the individual's profile, go to "Gallery," click "Add a Document," and include files in their original language. Ancestry.com supports a rich tapestry of family history from around the world.*

Question: Can I upload audio recordings or oral histories to Ancestry.com?

Answer: *Absolutely! Ancestry.com allows you to enrich your family history by uploading audio recordings or oral histories. Capture the voices and stories of your relatives to preserve the richness of your family's narrative. To upload audio recordings, follow these steps:*

1. *Access the person's profile in your family tree.*
2. *Navigate to the "Media" or "Gallery" section.*

3. *Choose "Upload Media" and select your audio file.*
4. *Provide a descriptive title and any relevant details.*
5. *Save the upload to link it to your ancestor's profile.*

Question: How do I ensure that my uploaded photos and documents are private or only accessible to specific family members?

Answer: *Protecting privacy is key. To ensure your media is private:*

1. *Adjust your tree's privacy settings to control who can view it.*
2. *When uploading, choose the privacy setting for each media item.*
3. *Utilize Ancestry.com's privacy features to share selectively with chosen family members.*

Question: Can I upload media that contains sensitive or private information about living individuals?

Answer: *Yes, but exercise caution. You can upload media with sensitive info but be mindful of privacy. Always respect living individuals' privacy and consider private sharing options on Ancestry.com.*

Question: Can I upload videos or home movies to Ancestry.com?

Answer: *Absolutely! Enrich your family history with videos. Upload them by following the same steps as photos and documents.*

Question: Can I upload media from social media platforms to Ancestry.com?

Answer: *Yes, you can upload media from social media platforms. Save the media to your device and then upload it to Ancestry.com.*

Question: Can I upload media for multiple family members at once?

Answer: *Yes, you can efficiently upload media for multiple family members on Ancestry.com. Begin by navigating to the "Family Tree" tab and selecting the desired person. Click on the "Media" tab within their profile. Here, you can upload photos, documents, and more by selecting "Add Media." Ensure your family's history is richly documented by seamlessly associating media with various family members in a single upload session.*

Question: How can I link a specific photo or document to a particular individual in my family tree?

Answer: *Linking photos or documents to specific individuals is a breeze on Ancestry.com. From the person's profile page, click on "Profile," then select "Add Media." Choose the relevant photo or document and link it to the individual by selecting their name from the dropdown menu. This ensures that your family tree becomes a visually engaging* *and comprehensive repository of your ancestors' stories.*

Question: Are there any restrictions on the file types I can upload?

Answer: *Ancestry.com supports various file types for media uploads, ensuring flexibility and accessibility. You can upload common image formats, such as JPEG and PNG, as well as document formats like PDF. Before uploading, verify that the file size is 15 MB or smaller to ensure a smooth and efficient process.*

Question: How can I ensure the photos/documents I upload are preserved for the long term?

Answer: *Rest assured, Ancestry.com is committed to preserving your uploaded photos and documents for the long term. The platform employs robust archival practices to safeguard your family history. Regularly back up your data, and consider downloading your tree periodically to ensure an additional layer of protection.*

Question: Is there a limit to the number of photos/documents I can upload?

Answer: *There's no need to limit your storytelling! Ancestry.com provides ample space for your family's journey. You can upload a substantial number of photos and documents to create a comprehensive narrative of your family history. Feel free to enrich your tree with visual elements that capture the essence of your ancestors' lives.*

Question: Can I add descriptions or captions to the photos/documents I upload?

Answer: *Absolutely! Enhance the storytelling of your family history by adding descriptions or captions to the photos and documents you upload on Ancestry.com.*

Provide context, share anecdotes, and create a more vivid picture of your ancestors' lives. Simply edit the media details to include meaningful descriptions that contribute to the richness of your family tree.

Question: Can I share the photos/documents I upload with other family members?

Answer: *Sharing your family history is a delightful experience on Ancestry.com. Easily share photos and documents with other family members by inviting them to your tree. Collaborate on building a collective narrative, fostering a sense of connection and shared heritage.*

Question: Is there a way to organize my uploaded photos/documents?

Answer: *Ancestry.com allows you to maintain order in your family history archive. Organize your uploaded photos and documents by creating albums. Group related media together to tell cohesive stories, making it easier to navigate and explore your family's rich heritage.*

Question: How can I add photos/documents to an existing album?

Answer: *To add photos or documents to an existing album on Ancestry.com, go to the*

"Family Tree" tab and select "Media." Click on the desired album, then choose "Add Media." Select the photos or documents you want to include, ensuring your family history albums continue to grow and tell a more complete story.

Question: Can I create separate albums for different branches of my family?

Answer: *Absolutely! Organize your family history creatively by creating separate albums for different branches of your family on Ancestry.com. From the "Family Tree" tab, navigate to "Media," select "Create a New Album," and customize it to represent distinct branches. This adds a visual dimension to your family history, making it more accessible and engaging.*

Question: Can I upload photos/documents that are physically stored in an album or binder?

Answer: *Yes, you can seamlessly digitize and upload photos or documents that are physically stored in albums or binders to Ancestry.com. Leverage the platform's upload* *functionality by selecting the relevant individual's profile, clicking on "Add Media," and choosing the desired files. Preserve and share your family's treasured memories with ease.*

Question: How can I view and manage the photos/documents I've uploaded on Ancestry.com?

Answer: *Managing your uploaded photos and documents is effortless on Ancestry.com. Simply go to the "Family Tree" tab, select "Media," and you'll find a comprehensive view of all your uploaded items.*

From here, you can easily edit details, move media between albums, and ensure your family history remains organized and accessible.

Question: Can I add photos/documents to my family tree directly from the Ancestry.com mobile app?

Answer: *Absolutely! Enriching your family tree with photos and documents is a mobile-friendly experience on Ancestry.com. Utilize the mobile app by selecting the individual's* *profile, tapping on "Add Media," and seamlessly uploading photos or documents directly from your mobile device. Share your family's story on the go!*

Question: Are there any privacy settings for the photos/documents I upload?

Answer: *Ancestry.com prioritizes your privacy. You can control who sees the photos and documents you upload by adjusting privacy settings. When uploading, choose the desired privacy level—whether for public view, restricted to your tree, or accessible only to specific individuals. This ensures a tailored and secure sharing experience*

Linking Media to Specific Individuals or Events

Question: How do I ensure that the uploaded media is properly linked to individuals in my family tree?

Answer: *Linking media is easy:*

1. *Access the person's profile.*

2. *Navigate to the "Media" or "Gallery" section.*
3. *Select "Link to Person" and choose the relevant individual.*

Question: Can I upload media for ancestors who lived in different time periods, such as the 18th or 19th century?

Answer: *Absolutely! There's no time limit. Upload media for ancestors from any period to create a comprehensive family history.*

Question: Can I create a timeline of media for a specific individual in the family tree?

Answer: *Yes, organize media into a timeline:*

1. *Create folders or albums for specific time periods or events.*
2. *Add media to each folder, creating a visual timeline.*

Question: Can I upload media for family members who were part of historical events or lived in significant periods?

> ***Answer:*** *Certainly! Share the historical significance of your family by uploading media related to their involvement in events or significant periods.*

Question: Can I upload media related to family traditions and cultural practices?

> ***Answer:*** *Absolutely! Celebrate your family's heritage by uploading media that reflects traditions and cultural practices.*

Question: Can I upload media for adopted family members or those related through marriage?

> ***Answer:*** *Yes, include all family members! Upload media for adopted members or those related through marriage to create a comprehensive family story.*

Question: Can I upload media for family members who emigrated from one country to another?

> ***Answer:*** *Yes, showcase the journey! Upload media illustrating the migration and experiences of family members who emigrated.*

Question: Can I upload media for family members who served in the military or participated in wars?

> ***Answer:*** *Absolutely! Honor military service by uploading photos, documents, or records showcasing their contributions.*

Question: Can I upload media for family members who were involved in historical movements or social causes?

> ***Answer:*** *Yes, highlight their impact! Share media illustrating their involvement in historical movements or social causes.*

Question: Can I upload media for family members who were pioneers or early settlers in a particular region?

> ***Answer:*** *Certainly! Upload media showcasing the pioneering spirit and contributions of your ancestors in specific regions.*

Question: Can I upload media for family members who were artists, writers, or musicians?

> ***Answer:*** *Absolutely! Showcase the creative talents of your family members by uploading media highlighting their artistic, literary, or musical endeavors.*

Question: How do I link media to specific individuals in my family tree on Ancestry.com?

> ***Answer:*** *Follow these steps:*
>
> 1. *Access the person's profile.*
> 2. *Navigate to the "Media" or "Gallery" section.*
> 3. *Select "Link to Person" and choose the relevant individual.*

Question: Can I link multiple photos or documents to one individual in my family tree?

Answer: *Yes, easily link multiple items:*

1. *Access the person's profile.*
2. *Navigate to the "Media" or "Gallery" section.*
3. *Select "Link to Person" and choose the relevant individual.*

Question: How do I remove or unlink media from an individual's profile on Ancestry.com?

Answer: *Unlinking is simple:*

1. *Access the person's profile.*
2. *Navigate to the "Media" or "Gallery" section.*
3. *Select the item and choose "Unlink from Person."*

Question: Can I link media to multiple individuals in my family tree?

Answer: *Yes, you can link media to multiple individuals:*

1. *Access the media item.*

2. *Choose "Link to Person" and select additional individuals.*

Question: Can I link census data and vital records to specific individuals in my family tree?

Answer: *Certainly! Linking is crucial for a comprehensive family history. Follow these steps:*

1. *Access the individual's profile.*
2. *Navigate to the "Facts" or "Timeline" section.*
3. *Add or edit events to link census data or vital records.*

Question: How do I link census data and vital records to individuals in my family tree on Ancestry.com?

Answer: *Follow these steps:*

1. *Access the individual's profile.*
2. *Navigate to the "Facts" or "Timeline" section.*
3. *Add or edit events, providing details from census data or vital records.*

Question: Can I link media and sources to the same individual in my family tree?

Answer: *Absolutely! Enhance your family tree by linking both media and sources to provide a comprehensive narrative.*

Question: Can I link memories to specific events or dates in the family tree?

Answer: *Absolutely! Enhance your family tree's storytelling by linking memories to specific events. In the individual's profile, click "Gallery" and select "Link to Family Tree." Choose the relevant event, creating a visual timeline that beautifully illustrates your family's journey.*

Question: Can I see who has viewed or interacted with the memories I've uploaded?

Answer: *While Ancestry.com doesn't provide a direct view count, you can gauge engagement through comments and reactions on shared memories. Encourage relatives to interact, creating a collaborative and shared family history experience.*

Question: Can I add memories to individuals who are not directly related to my family tree?

Answer: *Absolutely! Expand your family narrative by adding memories to individuals not directly related. Use the "Add a Person" feature to include extended family or close friends. Capture a holistic view of your family's connections and shared experiences.*

Question: How can I share memories with family members who are not on Ancestry.com?

Answer: *Share the joy of family memories with non-Ancestry.com users by exporting your family tree. Click "Tree Settings," select "Export Tree," and share the file with family members. They can explore your rich family history without needing an Ancestry.com account.*

Question: Can I import memories from other platforms or family history websites into Ancestry.com?

Answer: *While direct import features may vary, you can manually upload memories. Save* *images or documents from other platforms to your computer, then upload them to Ancestry.com by selecting "Add a Life Event" in the individual's profile.*

Question: Can I add memories to individuals who have not been added to the family tree yet?

Answer: *Certainly! Before adding someone to the family tree, go to the "Family Tree" tab, select "Add a Person," and provide basic details. Then, click "Gallery" on their profile to start documenting memories. Enrich your family tree as you expand your genealogical journey.*

Question: How can I ensure the privacy and security of the memories I upload on Ancestry.com?

Answer: *Ancestry.com prioritizes privacy. Adjust individual privacy settings by going to "Tree Settings" and selecting "Privacy Settings." Manage who can see living individuals' details and customize sharing options to ensure your family memories remain secure.*

Additional Resources:

1. *Ancestry.com - Uploading Media*
2. *Family History Fanatics - Ancestry Tips: A Trick To Link Photos to Events in Your...*
3. *Genealogist Help - How To Upload Photos And Documents In Ancestry?*
4. *Family Tree Magazine - Ancestry.com: Tips and Tricks for Beginners*
5. *PetaPixel - Ancestry.com's New Terms Allow it to Use Your Family... https://petapixel.com/2021/08/09/ancestry-coms-new-terms-allow-it-to-use-your-family-photos-for-anything/*
6. *Ancestry.com - Uploading Media Ancestry.com - Privacy Statement*
7. *YouTube - Uploading Pictures and Documents | Ancestry*
8. *Sequencing.com - Guide: How To Upload & Use Ancestry.com DNA data*
9. *Reddit - Why does Ancestry keep user-uploaded information*
10. *Family Tree Magazine - Ancestry.com: Tips and Tricks for Beginners*

Quick Links

Uploading Media: Photos, Stories, Audio, and Documents

Chapter 6
Research Tips and Strategies

Researching Difficult Ancestors

Question: How do I research difficult ancestors on Ancestry.com?

Answer: *Researching challenging ancestors requires a strategic approach. Begin by gathering all known information, creating a comprehensive timeline, and documenting family stories.*

Utilize Ancestry.com's search features*, employing various spellings and wildcard options.*

Explore specific record collections *relevant to your ancestor's location and time period.*

Leverage online forums and communities *to seek advice and collaborate with fellow researchers.*

Additionally, *explore the Ancestry.com Wiki and Learning Center for guidance on advanced search techniques, deciphering historical documents, and overcoming common research obstacles.*

Question: What should I do if I can't find any records for a difficult ancestor on Ancestry.com?

Answer: *When facing a research roadblock, reassess existing information and expand your search:*

1. ***Verify details:*** *Double-check names, dates, and locations for accuracy.*
2. ***Broaden search criteria:*** *Adjust filters and use wildcard characters to accommodate variations.*
3. ***Explore alternative records:*** *Investigate different collections beyond census and vital records.*
4. ***Seek community assistance:*** *Post queries on forums for insights and collaborate with other researchers.*
5. ***Consult the Ancestry.com Wiki and Learning Center****: Access resources to refine*

your research strategy and overcome challenges.

Question: Are there any specialized resources or databases that can aid in exploring specific ancestral lines, such as Native American or African American heritage?

Answer: *Dive deep into your heritage! Utilize Ancestry's diverse and specialized resources.*

1. *Explore Ancestry's specialized databases.*
2. *Use filters for ethnicity or region.*
3. *Access Native American or African American records*

Question: What strategies can I employ when researching ancestors with common surnames or limited identifying information?

Answer: *Navigate challenges with creativity! Employ strategic searching on Ancestry for success.*

1. *Use additional filters like birthdates or locations.*
2. *Employ wildcard characters in searches.*

3. *Explore alternative records for clues.*

Question: Are there any specialized resources or databases that can aid in exploring specific ancestral lines, such as Native American or African American heritage?

> ***Answer:*** *Dive deep into your heritage! Utilize Ancestry's diverse and specialized resources.*
>
> 1. *Explore Ancestry's specialized databases.*
> 2. *Use filters for ethnicity or region.*
> 3. *Access Native American or African American records*

Using Ancestry Wiki and Learning Center

Question: What are the benefits of utilizing Ancestry.com Wiki and Learning Center in exploring ancestral lines?

> ***Answer:*** *Empower your journey with knowledge! Utilize Ancestry's educational resources.*

1. *Visit Ancestry.com Wiki and Learning Center.*
2. *Explore guides, articles, and tutorials.*
3. *Learn about research techniques.*
4. *Gain insights into using Ancestry tools effectively.*

Question: What is the Ancestry.com Wiki, and how can I use it for my genealogy research?

Answer: *The Ancestry.com Wiki is a comprehensive resource offering:*

- ***Location-specific guidance:*** *Navigate to a specific region to access research tips and record explanations.*
- ***Research strategies:*** *Find expert advice on overcoming common genealogical challenges.*
- ***Record interpretation:*** *Gain insights into understanding and utilizing various historical records.*

Question: What is the Ancestry.com Learning Center, and how can it help me with my genealogy research?

Answer: *The Ancestry.com Learning Center provides:*

1. *Courses and webinars: Access educational content on advanced search techniques, record interpretation, and research strategies.*
2. *Skill enhancement: Elevate your genealogy skills through targeted learning modules.*
3. *Expert insights: Learn from seasoned genealogists to overcome research hurdles effectively.*

Question: How can I use the Ancestry.com Wiki to research a specific location for my ancestor's records?

Answer:

1. *Visit the Ancestry.com Wiki.*
2. *Navigate to the location of interest.*
3. *Explore resources, research tips, and record explanations tailored to that specific area.*

4. *Utilize the guidance to enhance your understanding of available records and research strategies.*

Question: What type of information can I find in the Ancestry.com Wiki for a specific location?

Answer: *The Ancestry.com Wiki for a specific location provides:*

1. ***Research guidance:*** *Tailored tips for effective genealogical research in that area.*
2. ***Record explanations:*** *Insights into the types of historical records available.*
3. ***Historical context:*** *Understand the cultural and historical background of the location.*
4. ***Community insights:*** *Benefit from shared experiences and advice from other researchers.*

Question: How do I access courses and webinars in the Ancestry.com Learning Center?

Answer:

1. *Visit the Ancestry.com Learning Center.*
2. *Browse available courses and webinars.*

3. *Select the desired topic or skill you want to enhance.*
4. *Enroll in courses to access valuable educational content and expert insights.*

Question: How can the Ancestry.com Learning Center help me improve my genealogy research skills?

Answer: *The Ancestry.com Learning Center is a valuable resource designed to enhance your genealogy skills. It offers a diverse range of courses and webinars covering advanced search techniques, record interpretation, and research strategies. Engaging with this educational hub provides a structured approach to refining your abilities.*

Whether you're a beginner or an experienced researcher, the Learning Center empowers you to navigate the complexities of genealogy with confidence. Explore the various modules and expert insights to elevate your understanding and make your genealogical journey more rewarding.

Leveraging Community and Online Forums

Question: How can I leverage community and online forums to aid in my exploration of ancestral lines?

Answer: *Unite with fellow explorers! Embrace the power of community in your ancestry quest.*

1. *Join Ancestry community forums.*
2. *Participate in discussions.*
3. *Seek advice and share experiences.*

Connect with experts and fellow researchers.

Question: How can I use Ancestry.com Wiki and Learning Center to research difficult ancestors?

Answer: *Maximize the Ancestry.com Wiki and Learning Center:*

- ***Ancestry.com Wiki:*** *Navigate to the Wiki to find location-specific research guidance, record explanations, and tips for overcoming challenges.*

- ***Learning Center:*** *Access courses and webinars covering advanced search techniques, record interpretation, and overcoming genealogical obstacles. Enhance your skills to tackle complex ancestral research effectively.*

Question: How can I leverage community and online forums to research difficult ancestors?

Answer: *Engage with the genealogy community:*

- ***Join forums:*** *Participate in Ancestry.com's community forums or external platforms.*
- ***Share details:*** *Clearly outline your research challenges, seeking advice and insights.*
- ***Collaborate:*** *Connect with researchers facing similar difficulties, fostering a collaborative approach to problem-solving.*

Respond and thank: *Acknowledge contributions, building a supportive network for ongoing assistance.*

Question: What are community and online forums, and how can they help with my genealogy research?

***Answer**: Community and online forums are platforms where genealogists connect, share insights, and seek assistance. Engaging in these forums:*

1. *Facilitates collaboration and knowledge exchange.*
2. *Provides access to diverse experiences and expertise.*
3. *Creates a supportive community for shared genealogical interests.*

Question: How do I find and join genealogy groups and forums on Ancestry.com?

***Answer:** Finding genealogy groups on Ancestry.com is easy:*

1. *Visit the "Community" section on Ancestry.com.*
2. *Explore the "Message Boards" or dedicated forums.*
3. *Browse topics or use the search bar to find specific groups.*

4. *Join discussions and contribute to the community.*

Question: How can I benefit from participating in genealogy forums?

Answer: *Participating in genealogy forums offers numerous benefits:*

1. *Gain insights and advice from experienced researchers.*
2. *Collaborate on challenging research problems.*
3. *Connect with distant relatives.*
4. *Stay updated on industry trends and research methodologies.*

Question: What etiquettes should I follow while participating in genealogy forums?

Answer: *When engaging in genealogy forums, adhere to these etiquettes:*

- *Be respectful and considerate of others' opinions.*
- *Provide accurate and constructive feedback.*
- *Stay on-topic and follow forum guidelines.*

- *Acknowledge and appreciate contributions from fellow researchers.*

Question: How can I search for specific topics or surnames within genealogy forums?

Answer: *To search for specific topics or surnames in genealogy forums:*

1. *Use the search bar within the forum section.*
2. *Enter relevant keywords, surnames, or topics.*
3. *Review search results and explore relevant discussions.*

Question: What should I do if I can't find an answer to my research question in the genealogy forums?

Answer: *If you can't find an answer in genealogy forums:*

1. *Revisit your research question for clarity.*
2. *Consider posting a detailed query with specific information.*
3. *Reach out to experienced members directly for personalized assistance.*

Question: How can I contribute my knowledge and research findings to genealogy forums?

Answer: *Contribute to genealogy forums by:*

1. *Sharing your research findings.*
2. *Providing helpful insights to others.*
3. *Participating in discussions and answering queries.*
4. *Collaborating on shared research projects.*

Question: Can I share images or documents in genealogy forums to support my research?

Answer: *Yes, you can share images or documents in genealogy forums to enhance your research:*

1. *Use the forum's "Upload" or "Attach" feature.*
2. *Provide context for shared materials.*
3. *Use images to illustrate research challenges or findings.*

Question: Can I communicate privately with other members in genealogy forums?

Answer: *Most genealogy forums allow private communication:*

1. *Check the forum's messaging or private chat features.*
2. *Respect privacy and obtain consent before initiating private conversations.*

Question: How can I keep track of forum discussions that interest me?

Answer: *To keep track of forum discussions:*

1. *Use the forum's "Follow" or "Subscribe" feature.*
2. *Receive notifications for updates on your tracked discussions.*

Question: Can I interact with forum members from different countries or regions?

Answer: *Yes, genealogy forums provide a global platform for interaction:*

1. *Explore international or region-specific forums.*

2. *Engage with researchers from diverse backgrounds.*
3. *Expand your network and exchange insights globally.*

Question: Are there forum discussions specifically for beginners in genealogy research?

Answer: *Yes, many genealogy forums host discussions for beginners:*

1. *Look for forums with "Beginner" or "Newbie" sections.*
2. *Participate in introductory discussions.*
3. *Seek advice from experienced members willing to guide beginners.*

Additional Resources:

1. *Overcoming Roadblocks in Your Research - Ancestry® Support*
2. *Ancestry.com Family History Wiki - YouTube*
3. *Using social media for genealogy research*
4. *Researching African American Ancestors - Ancestry® Support*
5. *Warning: I Am About to Vent About Ancestry.com - Reddit*

6. *How to Preserve and Share Your Genealogy Research*
7. *Message Boards on Ancestry®*
8. *Ancestry Community*

Chapter 7
Collaborating in Ancestry Community

Joining Ancestry Groups

Question: Why should I consider joining Ancestry.com groups?

Answer: *Joining Ancestry.com groups offers a vibrant community where you can connect with like-minded researchers, share discoveries, and receive valuable insights. By becoming part of these groups, you tap into a collective pool of knowledge, gaining access to varied perspectives that can illuminate your family history journey.*

Engaging with fellow genealogists fosters collaboration, turning what might seem like solitary research into a communal and rewarding experience.

Question: Can I join more than one Ancestry.com group?

Answer: *Absolutely! Ancestry.com encourages you to join multiple groups to expand your network and diversify your research connections. Each group may focus on different regions, surnames, or research methodologies. Embrace the opportunity to connect with various communities, enriching your genealogical exploration.*

Question: How do I find Ancestry.com groups that are relevant to my research?

Answer: *Discovering relevant groups is easy:*

1. *Navigate to the "Community" section on Ancestry.com.*
2. *Explore the "Groups" option to find a list of available groups.*
3. *Use the search bar to look for groups related to your research interests.*
4. *Join groups aligned with your geographical focus, surnames, or specific research challenges.*

Question: What kind of discussions happen in Ancestry.com groups?

Answer: *Ancestry.com groups host diverse discussions, including:*

1. *Sharing research findings and success stories.*
2. *Collaborating on challenging genealogical problems.*
3. *Seeking advice on specific regions or record types.*
4. *Engaging in conversations about best practices and methodologies.*

Question: How do I actively participate in group discussions?

Answer: *Actively engage in discussions by:*

1. *Introducing yourself and your research interests.*
2. *Responding to queries and sharing your insights.*
3. *Asking questions to seek advice or opinions.*

4. *Contributing positively to the community atmosphere.*

Question: Can I ask for help with my specific genealogy challenges in a group?

Answer: *Absolutely! Ancestry.com groups are supportive communities where seeking help for specific genealogy challenges is encouraged. Share details about your research roadblocks, and fellow group members are likely to offer guidance, resources, or solutions.*

Question: How can I make sure I'm following the group's guidelines and being respectful?

Answer: *To ensure you follow group guidelines:*

1. *Read the group's rules and guidelines before participating.*
2. *Be respectful of others' opinions and research approaches.*
3. *Stay on-topic and contribute constructively.*
4. *If unsure, ask for clarification from group moderators.*

Question: Can I leave a group if I'm no longer interested?

> ***Answer:*** *Yes, you can leave a group at any time. Navigate to the group's page, find the "Join Group" button (which indicates you are a member), and click to leave. This allows you to tailor your group memberships based on your evolving research interests.*

Question: How do I receive notifications from the groups I've joined?

> ***Answer:*** *To receive notifications:*
>
> 1. *Join the group you're interested in.*
> 2. *Adjust notification settings in the group, typically found in the group's settings.*
> 3. *Choose to receive updates on new posts, comments, or other relevant activities.*

Question: Can I invite others to join an Ancestry.com group?

> ***Answer:*** *Unfortunately, as of the provided information, Ancestry.com doesn't explicitly mention a feature for members to invite others*

to groups. Group participation typically involves members joining voluntarily.

Question: How can I ask questions about my genealogy research in the Ancestry.com Community?

Answer: *To ask questions in the Ancestry.com Community:*

1. *Navigate to the "Community" section on Ancestry.com.*
2. *Click on "Ask the Community" or a similar option.*
3. *Enter your question, providing relevant details.*
4. *Submit your question and await responses from the community.*

Question: How can I answer questions in the Ancestry.com Community?

Answer: *Answering questions in the Ancestry.com Community is straightforward:*

1. *Browse through the list of open questions.*
2. *Click on a question that aligns with your expertise.*

3. *Provide a detailed and helpful response based on your knowledge.*
4. *Engage in positive and constructive interactions.*

Question: Can I ask for help with specific individuals or family lines in the Ancestry.com Community?

Answer: *Yes, you can seek assistance with specific individuals or family lines in the Ancestry.com Community. When asking for help, provide relevant details such as names, dates, and locations to facilitate more accurate and targeted responses.*

Question: How do I search for questions related to my research interests?

Answer: *To search for questions related to your research interests:*

1. *Use the search bar in the Ancestry.com Community.*
2. *Enter keywords, surnames, or locations relevant to your research.*

3. *Review search results to find questions aligning with your interests.*

Question: What should I do if I come across a question that I can answer?

Answer: *If you come across a question you can answer:*

1. *Click on the question to view its details.*
2. *Craft a detailed and accurate response.*
3. *Share your insights to assist the community.*
4. *Ensure your answer is respectful and contributes positively.*

Question: Can I provide additional information or clarification to an existing answer?

Answer: *Yes, you can provide additional information or clarification to an existing answer:*

1. *Locate the answer you wish to enhance.*
2. *Add a comment providing the necessary details or clarifications.*
3. *Contribute to a more comprehensive understanding of the topic.*

Question: How can I make sure my answer is accurate before posting it?

Answer: *Ensure the accuracy of your answer by:*

1. *Double-checking facts and details.*
2. *Cross-referencing information with reliable sources.*
3. *Seeking input from other community members if uncertain.*
4. *Conveying your response in a clear and concise manner.*

Question: What if I don't know the answer to a question?

Answer: *If you encounter a question, you don't know the answer to, don't worry! The Ancestry.com Community is a supportive space, and honesty is appreciated. You can still contribute by sharing your thoughts or insights, and fellow researchers may provide valuable input. Remember, learning and* *exploring together is what makes the community thrive.*

Question: Can I receive notifications when someone answers my question?

Answer: *Absolutely! Stay engaged by enabling notifications. After posting a question, ensure your account settings include email or platform notifications. This way, you'll be promptly informed when someone responds, allowing you to stay connected and responsive to the evolving discussions.*

Question: How do I mark a question as "answered"?

Answer: *Once your question receives a satisfying response, mark it as "answered" to help others quickly identify resolved inquiries. Locate the "Mark as Answered" or similar option near your question. Your proactive involvement in marking questions contributes to a well-organized and efficient community.*

Question: What if I want to follow up on a question I asked earlier?

Answer: *Following up on your questions is encouraged. Check for responses regularly and engage in the conversation. If you need more details or clarification, reply directly to the answers received. Continuous communication ensures a dynamic and collaborative research environment.*

Sharing Research Findings and Stories

Question: How can I share my family history discoveries with others?

Answer: *Ancestry.com offers several ways to share your family history discoveries:*

Publish your family tree: *Share your family tree publicly or with specific individuals, allowing others to explore your research and contribute to the family history.*

Create stories and timelines: *Use Ancestry's storytelling tools to add narratives, photos, and timelines to your family tree, making your* *discoveries more engaging and meaningful for others.*

Publish blog posts: *Share your research journey, discoveries, and insights through Ancestry's blog platform, reaching a wider audience and contributing to the genealogy community.*

Connect with family members*: Share your findings directly with family members, fostering connections and building a sense of shared history.*

Participate in online forums: *Share your stories and discoveries on online genealogy forums, connecting with others who share your interests and fostering a passion for family history.*

**** These questions and answers provide a comprehensive overview of how you can discover your family history using the various tools and resources available on Ancestry.com. Remember, the journey of discovering your family history is a continuous learning process. Utilize the available resources, ask for help when needed, and enjoy the rewarding experience of uncovering your heritage.*

Question: Can I share photos and documents along with my research stories on Ancestry.com?

> ***Answer:*** *Absolutely! Enhance your stories by attaching photos and documents. While sharing your story, look for options like "Attach File" or "Add Photo." Uploading visual elements enriches your narrative, making it more compelling and providing a holistic view of your family history.*

Question: How can I find and read stories shared by other researchers in the Ancestry.com Community?

> ***Answer:*** *Discovering stories from fellow researchers is simple. Explore the community platform and look for sections like "Stories" or "Shared Findings." Browse through posts or use search functionalities to find captivating narratives that resonate with your research interests.*

Question: Can I comment on stories shared by others in the Ancestry.com Community?

> ***Answer:*** *Absolutely! Engage with the community by leaving thoughtful comments on stories that pique your interest. Share your insights, ask questions, or express appreciation. Building connections through positive interactions strengthens the collaborative spirit of the community.*

Question: How can I show appreciation for a story that I find particularly interesting or helpful?

> ***Answer:*** *If you come across a story that resonates with you, show appreciation! Look for options like "Like," "Upvote," or "Thumbs Up" near the story. Your acknowledgment not only encourages the storyteller but also fosters a culture of support within the Ancestry.com Community.*

Question: What should I include in my research findings or stories to make them more engaging?

> ***Answer:*** *Craft engaging stories by including vivid details. Share names, dates, and locations, but also delve into the personalities, challenges, and triumphs of your ancestors. Paint a narrative that captivates readers and brings the past to life, making your research findings more compelling.*

Question: How can I ensure the accuracy of the information I share in my research stories?

> ***Answer:*** *Prioritize accuracy by cross-referencing information with reliable sources. Verify facts, dates, and relationships before sharing. If you're uncertain, seek input from the community. Ensuring accuracy not only upholds the integrity of your story but also contributes to the overall credibility of shared research.*

Question: Can I edit or update a story after I've posted it?

> ***Answer:*** *Yes, you can refine your stories even after posting. Locate the "Edit" option near your published story and make necessary updates. This flexibility ensures that your narratives remain accurate and reflective of your evolving research.*

Question: How can I get feedback on my research findings or stories from the Ancestry.com Community?

> ***Answer:*** *Actively seek feedback by encouraging comments and discussions on your posts. Pose specific questions or request input on aspects of your research. Embracing feedback enhances the collaborative nature of the community, fostering a culture of shared learning and improvement.*

Question: Is there a way to organize and categorize the stories I share on Ancestry.com?

> ***Answer:*** *Organize your stories by utilizing features like tags or categories, if available. This ensures that your contributions are easily searchable and accessible to others interested in similar topics. An organized approach enhances the overall usability of the community platform.*

Additional Resources:

1. *Ancestry.com Community Rules*
2. *Join Ancestry®*
3. *Family Groups on Ancestry®*
4. *Ancestry Terms and Conditions*
5. *Finding Your Membership Status and Billing Details on Ancestry*
6. *Messaging on Ancestry®*
7. *AncestryDNA® Communities*
8. *Ancestry® Family History Learning Hub*
9. *DNA Surveys FAQs*
10. *AncestryClassroom | Home*

Quick Links

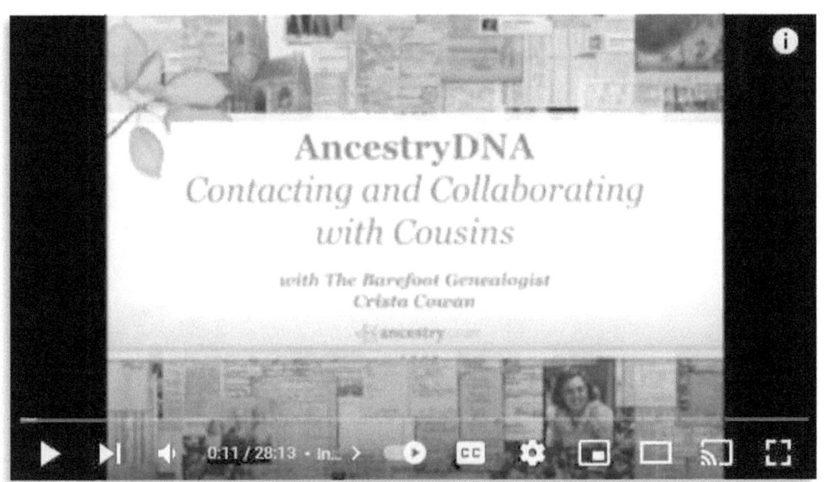
AncestryDNA
Contacting and Collaborating
with Cousins
with The Barefoot Genealogist
Crista Cowan
ancestry
0:11 / 28:13

Chapter 8

Advanced Features and DNA Testing

Exploring Advanced Ancestry Features

Question: What are some advanced features on Ancestry.com that I can explore to enhance my genealogy research?

Answer: *Ancestry.com offers several advanced features to enrich your genealogy journey. Explore the Ancestry.com Learning Hub for in-depth courses, dive into the Ancestry.com Catalog to discover unique collections, and leverage the Research Wiki for valuable insights. Utilize Record Hints to uncover new information, manage your family tree on-the-go with the Family Tree app, and engage with the community forum to benefit from diverse perspectives.*

Question: How do I use Record Hints on Ancestry.com to discover new information about my ancestors?

> ***Answer:*** *Record Hints on Ancestry.com provide automated suggestions for potential matches in their vast databases. To use them effectively, regularly check your profile's hint notifications. Review suggested records, compare details, and accept or reject the hints based on relevance. This feature aids in discovering previously unknown information about your ancestors.*

Question: What is the Ancestry.com Catalog, and how can it assist me in my research?

> ***Answer:*** *The Ancestry.com Catalog is a comprehensive repository of their record collections. Use it to explore diverse resources, filter collections by location and type, and discover unique documents relevant to your research. The catalog enhances your ability to access specific records crucial for building your family tree.*

Question: How can the Family Tree app help me manage my family tree while I'm on the go?

Answer: *The Family Tree app enables you to manage your family tree conveniently from anywhere. Stay connected to your research by adding, editing, or updating information on-the-go. Access your family tree, review hints, and make real-time contributions, ensuring your genealogy journey remains seamless and flexible.*

Question: How can I access online genealogy classes on Ancestry.com?

Answer: *Accessing online genealogy classes on Ancestry.com is easy. Visit the Ancestry.com Learning Center, explore the available courses, and enroll in those of interest. The Learning Center provides a wealth of knowledge, allowing you to enhance your genealogy skills at your own pace.*

Question: Can I access the Ancestry.com Learning Center courses anytime, or are they scheduled?

> ***Answer:*** *You can access Ancestry.com Learning Center courses at any time. The courses are designed to accommodate your schedule, providing flexibility for learners. Explore the diverse topics and engage in genealogy education whenever it suits you best.*

Question: How can I benefit from the insights and experiences of other genealogists in the Ancestry.com community?

> ***Answer:*** *Engage with the Ancestry.com community forum to benefit from the collective wisdom of fellow genealogists. Pose questions, share experiences, and participate in discussions. This collaborative space fosters a supportive environment, allowing you to gain valuable insights and diverse perspectives.*

Question: What are some topics I can explore in the Ancestry.com Community forum?

> ***Answer:*** *The Ancestry.com Community forum covers a broad spectrum of genealogy-related topics. Explore threads on research methodologies, specific record collections, regional genealogy, and more. Engaging in discussions on these diverse topics allows you to broaden your knowledge and connect with like-minded researchers.*

Integrating DNA Testing with Your Family History

Question: How can I integrate DNA testing with my family history research on Ancestry.com?

> ***Answer:*** *Integrating DNA testing with your family history research on Ancestry.com opens new avenues of exploration. Learn more about your genetic heritage, connect with relatives, and validate ancestral relationships. Utilize features like Shared Ancestor Hints to discover common ancestors with your DNA matches.*

Question: What is the benefit of integrating DNA testing with my Ancestry.com family tree?

Answer: *Integrating DNA testing with your Ancestry.com family tree provides a holistic view of your genealogy. It helps confirm relationships, identify shared ancestors, and break through genealogical brick walls. This integration enhances the depth and accuracy of your family history research.*

Question: How do I link my DNA test results to my Ancestry.com account?

Answer: *Linking your DNA test results to your Ancestry.com account is a straightforward process. Follow the platform's prompts to connect your DNA kit to your existing family tree or create a new one. This linkage allows Ancestry.com to provide personalized insights based on your genetic data.*

Question: How do I identify shared ancestors with my DNA matches on Ancestry.com?

> ***Answer:*** *Identifying shared ancestors with your DNA matches involves examining family trees and shared connections. Explore the family trees of your matches, compare ancestral information, and look for common relatives. Shared Ancestor Hints may also highlight potential shared ancestors, simplifying the process.*

Question: Can I communicate with my DNA matches on Ancestry.com?

> ***Answer:*** *Yes, you can communicate with your DNA matches on Ancestry.com. Use the platform's messaging system to reach out to matches, inquire about shared ancestors, and exchange information. Collaborating with DNA matches enhances your ability to build a more comprehensive family tree.*

Question: How do I send a message to my DNA matches on Ancestry.com?

> ***Answer:*** *Sending a message to your DNA matches on Ancestry.com is easy. Visit the match's profile, click on the messaging option, and compose your message. Introduce yourself, share relevant family information, and express your interest in exploring shared ancestry.*

Question: Can DNA testing help me break through genealogical brick walls?

> ***Answer:*** *Yes, DNA testing can be a powerful tool to break through genealogical brick walls. By identifying genetic connections with relatives, you may uncover previously unknown branches of your family tree and overcome challenges in traditional paper trail research.*

Question: How do I ensure privacy when integrating DNA testing with my Ancestry.com family tree?

Answer: *Ancestry.com prioritizes user privacy. Adjust your DNA test settings to control the visibility of your genetic data. You can choose to share your results with specific individuals or keep them private. Review and customize your privacy preferences in the DNA settings section of your Ancestry.com account.*

Question: Can I upload DNA test results from other testing companies to Ancestry.com?

Answer: *While Ancestry.com primarily uses their own DNA database, you can transfer DNA test results from other companies to enhance your matches. Utilize third-party tools like GEDmatch for broader connections. However, note that not all features, like Shared Ancestor Hints, may be available for transferred results.*

Question: How can I leverage DNA testing to enhance my exploration of ancestral lines?

Answer: *Unlock the secrets in your genes! Dive into the fascinating world of AncestryDNA.*

1. *Order an AncestryDNA kit.*
2. *Follow instructions to provide a saliva sample.*
3. *Activate your kit online.*
4. *Receive DNA results.*

Explore DNA matches and ethnicity estimate.

[Understanding Genetic Genealogy]

Question: What steps do I take to identify shared ancestors with my DNA matches on Ancestry.com?

Answer: *Uncovering shared ancestors through DNA matches on Ancestry.com is a thrilling journey. Follow these steps:*

1. ***Access DNA Matches:*** *Log in to Ancestry.com and navigate to the "DNA Matches" section.*
2. ***Explore Shared Ancestor Hints:*** *Ancestry provides Shared Ancestor Hints based on family trees. Explore these hints to identify potential common ancestors.*
3. ***Examine Family Trees:*** *Review the linked family trees of your DNA matches. Look for shared surnames, locations, and specific individuals.*
4. ***Initiate Communication:*** *Reach out to your DNA matches through Ancestry's messaging system. Collaborate on family history to unravel shared ancestors.*

Building connections with your matches not only enriches your family history but also brings joy to the journey of discovery.

Question: Can I communicate with my DNA matches on Ancestry.com?

Answer: *Absolutely! Communicating with your DNA matches on Ancestry.com is a key aspect of collaborative genealogy. Here's how:*

1. ***Access DNA Matches:*** *Log in to Ancestry.com and visit the "DNA Matches" section.*
2. ***Choose a Match:*** *Select a DNA match you want to communicate with.*
3. ***Initiate Message:*** *On your match's profile, click the "Message" button.*
4. ***Craft Your Message:*** *Write a friendly introduction, express your interest in shared ancestry, and provide relevant family details.*
5. ***Send Your Message:*** *Click "Send" to start the conversation.*

Open communication fosters collaboration, helping you unravel family connections. Happy connecting.

Question: How do I send a message to my DNA matches on Ancestry.com?

Answer: *Sending a message to your DNA matches on Ancestry.com is easy. Visit the match's profile, click on the messaging option, and compose your message. Introduce yourself, share relevant family information,* *and express your interest in exploring shared ancestry.*

Question: Can DNA testing help me break through genealogical brick walls?

> ***Answer:*** *Yes, DNA testing can be a powerful tool to break through genealogical brick walls. By identifying genetic connections with relatives, you may uncover previously unknown branches of your family tree and overcome challenges in traditional paper trail research.*

Question: How do I ensure privacy when integrating DNA testing with my Ancestry.com family tree?

> ***Answer:*** *Ancestry.com prioritizes your privacy. To ensure a secure integration of DNA testing with your family tree, follow these steps:*
>
> 1. ***Adjust Privacy Settings:*** *Log in to Ancestry.com and navigate to your account settings. Adjust privacy preferences to control who can view your DNA results and family tree.*

2. ***Share Selectively:*** *When connecting with DNA matches, share information selectively. You can choose to reveal specific details without compromising your entire family tree.*
3. ***Communicate Privately:*** *Use Ancestry's messaging system to communicate with matches while keeping sensitive information within the platform.*
4. ***Regularly Review Settings:*** *Periodically review and update your privacy settings to align with your comfort level.*

By navigating Ancestry.com's privacy features, you can confidently explore your genetic heritage without compromising personal information.

Question: Can I upload DNA test results from other testing companies to Ancestry.com?

Answer: *While Ancestry.com primarily uses their own DNA database, you can transfer DNA test results from other companies to enhance your matches. Utilize third-party tools like GEDmatch for broader connections. However, note that not all features, like Shared*

Ancestor Hints, may be available for transferred results.

Question: What is genetic genealogy and how can it enhance my family history research?

***Answer**: Genetic genealogy is a groundbreaking approach that leverages DNA testing to explore familial connections and ancestry. By combining traditional genealogical research with DNA analysis, you can:*

1. ***Confirm Lineages:** DNA testing provides empirical evidence to verify documented family connections.*
2. ***Discover New Relatives:** Connect with unknown relatives who share common ancestors, expanding your family network.*
3. ***Break Through Brick Walls:** Overcome challenging genealogical puzzles by identifying genetic matches that bridge gaps in your research.*
4. ***Explore Ethnicity:** Gain insights into your ethnic background, enriching your understanding of your heritage.*

Embrace genetic genealogy as a complementary tool to traditional research, opening new avenues for discovery in your family history journey.

Question: How does genetic genealogy work on Ancestry.com?

***Answer**: Genetic genealogy on Ancestry.com involves analyzing your DNA to uncover familial connections and enhance your family history research. Start by taking the AncestryDNA test, which compares your DNA with others in the extensive AncestryDNA database. As your results come in, explore your DNA matches, individuals who share genetic similarities with you.*

Ancestry.com estimates the degree of relatedness, helping you identify potential relatives. Utilize the platform's tools and features to build a comprehensive family tree, combining genetic evidence with traditional research.

Collaborate with DNA matches, review shared ancestors, and unravel new branches in your family history. The integration of genetic data enriches your understanding of familial relationships, making your genealogical journey more rewarding.

Question: What is the Shared Ancestor Hints feature on Ancestry.com DNA?

Answer: *The Shared Ancestor Hints feature on Ancestry.com DNA is a powerful tool that identifies common ancestors between you and your DNA matches. When exploring your DNA matches, Ancestry.com provides hints highlighting shared ancestors with your matches. To use this feature:*

1. ***Access Your DNA Matches:*** *Log in to Ancestry.com and navigate to your DNA results.*
2. ***Filter by Common Ancestors:*** *Use the Common Ancestors filter to focus on matches with shared ancestors.*
3. ***Explore Hints:*** *Click on a match's name to view potential shared ancestors and explore the suggested connections.*
4. ***Collaborate with Matches:*** *Reach out to your matches to exchange information and*

build a more detailed family tree collaboratively.

Shared Ancestor Hints streamline the process of identifying common family ties, fostering collaboration with your DNA matches in uncovering shared ancestral roots.

Question: Can genetic genealogy help me find relatives from different parts of the world?

Answer: *Absolutely! Genetic genealogy transcends geographical boundaries, allowing you to connect with relatives from diverse parts of the world.*

Ancestry.com's global DNA database enables you to discover matches with shared genetic heritage, even if your ancestors originated from different continents. Embrace the opportunity to explore your global family network by engaging with DNA matches, exchanging information, and uncovering common ancestors.

The collaborative nature of genetic genealogy on Ancestry.com fosters a worldwide community of individuals united by a shared interest in family history.

Emphasize the interconnectedness of your familial roots, celebrating the diversity that enriches your genealogical journey.

Question: How do I interpret DNA match information on Ancestry.com?

Answer: *Interpreting DNA match information on Ancestry.com is an exciting part of your genealogical journey. When you receive DNA match results, follow these steps for a meaningful interpretation:*

1. ***Review Relationship Estimates:*** *Ancestry.com provides estimates of your relationship with DNA matches. Understand the degrees of kinship indicated, ranging from close family to distant cousins.*
2. ***Explore Shared Ancestors:*** *Utilize the Shared Ancestor Hints feature to identify common ancestors with matches. Investigate family trees and shared connections to deepen your understanding.*
3. ***Consider Additional Tools:*** *Ancestry.com offers tools like ThruLines, which visually displays potential ancestral connections. Explore these tools to uncover additional insights.*

4. ***Collaborate with Matches:*** *Initiate communication with matches to exchange information, stories, and details about your family history. Collaborative efforts often unveil hidden connections and enrich your research.*

Embrace the discovery process and remember that each DNA match holds a piece of your unique family puzzle.

Question: Can I explore my genetic ethnicity on Ancestry.com?

Answer: *Absolutely! Ancestry.com provides a fascinating journey into your genetic ethnicity, offering insights into your ancestral origins. Once you've taken the AncestryDNA test, follow these steps to explore your genetic ethnicity:*

1. ***Access Your DNA Results:*** *Log in to Ancestry.com and navigate to your DNA results page.*
2. ***Explore Ethnicity Estimates:*** *Look for the section that provides Ethnicity Estimates. Click to view a breakdown of your genetic heritage, highlighting regions and percentages associated with your ancestry.*

3. ***Detailed Insights:*** *Dive deeper into each ethnicity category to access detailed information about the regions and populations that contribute to your genetic makeup.*
4. ***Learn and Share:*** *Gain a deeper understanding of your cultural and ancestral background. Share these discoveries with family members to create a richer collective narrative of your heritage.*

Exploring your genetic ethnicity on Ancestry.com is an enlightening and educational experience that adds a vibrant dimension to your family history journey.

Question: How can I use genetic genealogy to confirm relationships?

Answer: *Genetic genealogy is a powerful tool for confirming relationships in your family history. To use it effectively on Ancestry.com:*

1. ***Compare DNA Matches:*** *Review shared DNA matches with individuals you believe are related. Consistent DNA matches across multiple relatives strengthen the evidence of shared ancestry.*

2. ***Shared Ancestor Hints:*** *Leverage the Shared Ancestor Hints feature to identify common ancestors with DNA matches. This shared lineage provides additional confirmation of relationships.*
3. ***ThruLines and Genetic Communities:*** *Utilize Ancestry.com's ThruLines and Genetic Communities features to visualize and confirm connections. ThruLines displays potential ancestors based on DNA matches and family trees.*
4. ***Collaborate and Verify:*** *Communicate with DNA matches to cross-verify family connections. Sharing family stories and documents enhances the confirmation process.*

   Embrace the collaborative nature of genetic genealogy on Ancestry.com, using DNA evidence to solidify and confirm relationships in your family tree.

Question: What should I do if I find a potential relative through genetic genealogy?

Answer: *Discovering a potential relative through genetic genealogy is an exciting* *moment in your family history journey. Here's what you can do:*

1. ***Initiate Communication:*** *Reach out to the potential relative through Ancestry.com's messaging system. Express your interest in exploring the shared family connection.*
2. ***Share Information:*** *Exchange family stories, photos, and documents to deepen your understanding of the familial link. Collaborate to build a more comprehensive family tree.*
3. ***Collaborate on Research:*** *Work together to verify and expand your family history. Combine your research efforts to uncover additional details, confirming the accuracy of the shared connection.*
4. ***Celebrate Discoveries:*** *Embrace the newfound family connection, celebrate shared heritage, and create a meaningful bond with your newfound relative.*

The key is open communication and collaborative exploration to enrich both of your family histories.

Question: Can I use genetic genealogy to trace my lineage back through many generations?

Answer: Yes, genetic genealogy on Ancestry.com can be a powerful tool for tracing your lineage back through many generations. Follow these steps:

1. ***Build a Robust Family Tree:*** *Create a comprehensive family tree on Ancestry.com, incorporating as many known relatives as possible.*
2. ***Take the AncestryDNA Test:*** *Complete the AncestryDNA test to add genetic data to your family tree.*
3. ***Explore DNA Matches:*** *Review your DNA matches on Ancestry.com, paying attention to shared ancestors and potential familial connections.*
4. ***ThruLines and Genetic Communities:*** *Utilize features like ThruLines and Genetic Communities to visualize ancestral connections and lineage pathways.*
5. ***Collaborate with Matches:*** *Communicate and collaborate with DNA matches to fill in gaps, verify connections, and uncover ancestral details.*

Through a combination of traditional genealogical research and genetic evidence, you can trace your lineage back through many generations, uncovering the rich tapestry of your family history.

Question: How can I learn more about genetic genealogy and its applications?

Answer: *Delving into genetic genealogy and its applications is an exciting and continuous learning process. To enhance your understanding:*

1. ***Educational Resources:*** *Explore Ancestry.com's DNA Learning Hub, which provides in-depth articles, guides, and tutorials on genetic genealogy.*
2. ***Community Forums:*** *Engage with the Ancestry.com community through forums and discussion groups. Share experiences, ask questions, and learn from the insights of others.*
3. ***Webinars and Workshops:*** *Attend webinars and workshops offered by Ancestry.com to gain practical insights and tips from experts in the field.*

4. ***Read Books and Publications:*** *Expand your knowledge by reading books and publications dedicated to genetic genealogy. Ancestry.com's library and external resources can offer valuable insights.*
5. ***Stay Updated:*** *Keep abreast of advancements in genetic genealogy through regular updates from Ancestry.com and other reputable sources.*

Embrace the learning journey and remember that each discovery contributes to a deeper appreciation of your family history.

Quick Links

Chapter 9
Ensuring Data Security and Privacy

Best Practices for Securing Personal Data

Question: How does Ancestry.com ensure the accuracy of its information?

Answer: *Ancestry.com employs a team of experts to curate and verify the historical records in its database. Additionally, the platform encourages users to contribute information and corrections, which are then reviewed by the research team. While inaccuracies may still exist, Ancestry.com strives to provide the most accurate and reliable information possible.*

Question: Are there any privacy concerns associated with using Ancestry.com?

> ***Answer:*** *Ancestry.com takes user privacy seriously and offers various controls and settings to manage how your information is shared. You can choose what information is displayed on your profile, control who can contact you, and opt-out of DNA research. Additionally, Ancestry.com is compliant with data privacy regulations, such as the General Data Protection Regulation (GDPR).*

Question: What are some basic best practices for securing my Ancestry.com account?

> ***Answer:*** *To enhance the security of your Ancestry.com account:*
>
> 1. ***Strong Password:*** *Create a robust password with a combination of letters, numbers, and symbols.*
> 2. ***Two-Factor Authentication (FA):*** *Enable two-factor authentication for an additional layer of security.*
> 3. ***Regular Password Updates:*** *Change your password periodically to prevent unauthorized access.*

4. ***Secure Wi-Fi:*** *Use a secure and private Wi-Fi network when accessing Ancestry.com to prevent data interception.*
5. ***Be Cautious:*** *Avoid sharing login credentials and be wary of phishing attempts.*

For detailed instructions on creating a strong password and enabling two-factor authentication, refer to Ancestry's Security of Personal Information and Creating an Ancestry® Password.

Additional Resources:

1. *Ancestry® Privacy Statement*
2. *Security of Personal Information - Ancestry*
3. *Creating an Ancestry® Password*

Question: How can I create a strong and secure password for my Ancestry.com account?

Answer: *Creating a robust password is essential for securing your Ancestry.com account. Start by crafting a password that combines uppercase and lowercase letters, numbers, and special characters. Avoid easily guessable information like birthdays or* *common words. Aim for a passphrase that is memorable but not easily predictable. For example, you can string together the first letters of a favorite quote or song lyrics, mixing in numbers and symbols. Ensure your password is at least 12 characters long. Regularly update your password and refrain from using the same one across multiple platforms to enhance security.*

Question: What is two-factor authentication (FA), and why should I enable it?

Answer: *Two-factor authentication (2FA) adds an extra layer of protection to your Ancestry.com account. Once enabled, 2FA requires you to verify your identity with a second method, typically a code sent to your mobile device. Enabling 2FA significantly enhances the security of your account by preventing unauthorized access, even if someone obtains your password. This additional step adds a crucial barrier, making it more challenging for potential intruders to compromise your account.*

Question: How do I enable two-factor authentication (FA) for my Ancestry.com account?

Answer: *Enabling two-factor authentication (2FA) on your Ancestry.com account is straightforward. Follow these steps:*

1. *Log in to your Ancestry.com account.*
2. *Navigate to your account settings, usually found in the upper-right corner.*
3. *Look for the security or privacy settings.*
4. *Find the option for two-factor authentication.*
5. *Follow the on-screen instructions to link your account with a mobile device.*
6. *Once linked, you may receive a verification code on your mobile device during login. Enter this code to complete the 2FA setup.*

Question: Is it safe to use public Wi-Fi when accessing Ancestry.com?

Answer: *While using public Wi-Fi, exercise caution when accessing sensitive information on Ancestry.com. Public networks may pose security risks, making it advisable to avoid* *logging in or accessing personal data in such environments. If necessary, consider using a Virtual Private Network (VPN) to encrypt your connection and enhance security. Always prioritize the safety of your data by accessing Ancestry.com on secure, private networks to reduce the risk of unauthorized access.*

Question: How can I protect my personal data when sharing it with other family members on Ancestry.com?

Answer: *Safeguarding your data while collaborating with family is crucial. Ancestry.com offers privacy settings allowing you to control who views your family history information. Before sharing, review and adjust privacy settings to limit access to specific individuals. Encourage open communication with family members, emphasizing the importance of respecting privacy settings. Educate them on responsible data handling and the significance of maintaining the confidentiality of shared family information.*

Question: What should I do if I suspect unauthorized access to my Ancestry.com account?

> ***Answer:*** *If you suspect unauthorized access, take immediate action to secure your account. Change your password to a strong, unique combination of characters. Enable two-factor authentication (2FA) for an additional layer of security. Review your account activity for any unfamiliar changes or additions. If concerns persist, contact Ancestry.com support promptly, providing details of your suspicions. They can assist in investigating and securing your account against potential unauthorized access.*

Question: Can I delete my Ancestry.com account if I no longer want to use the platform?

> ***Answer:*** *Yes, you can delete your Ancestry.com account if you decide not to continue using the platform. To do so, follow these steps:*
>
> 1. *Log in to your Ancestry.com account.*
> 2. *Go to your account settings or profile options.*

3. *Look for an option related to account deletion or closure.*
4. *Follow the on-screen instructions to initiate the account deletion process.*
5. *Confirm your decision, and your account will be permanently deleted.*

Question: How can I ensure the security of physical documents and photos I upload to Ancestry.com?

Answer: *Ensuring the security of uploaded documents and photos is essential. Before uploading, consider digitizing physical documents using reputable scanning tools. Remove or redact sensitive information, focusing on names and dates. When uploading, use Ancestry.com's privacy settings to control who can access these materials. Regularly review and update privacy settings as needed. Keep local backups of your digital files for added security, ensuring your valuable family history materials remain protected.*

Question: What should I do if I encounter suspicious or phishing emails related to Ancestry.com?

Answer: *If you receive suspicious or phishing emails related to Ancestry.com, exercise caution. Avoid clicking on any links or providing personal information. Ancestry.com typically communicates important information through your account inbox rather than email. Verify the email's authenticity by checking for grammatical errors, sender details, and unusual requests. Report suspicious emails to Ancestry.com's support or customer service. Educate yourself on common phishing signs to enhance your email security and protect your Ancestry.com account from potential threats.*

Question: Can I share my Ancestry.com login credentials with others?

Answer: *It's strongly discouraged to share your Ancestry.com login credentials. Protect the security of your family history information by keeping your login details confidential. Instead of sharing credentials, consider using Ancestry.com's collaboration features, such as* *inviting family members to join your tree. This way, they can contribute without compromising the security of your account. Upholding individual accounts ensures better control, privacy, and the integrity of your family history data.*

Understanding Ancestry.com's Privacy Policies

Question: Why is data security important when using Ancestry.com?

Answer: *Data security is crucial when using Ancestry.com to safeguard your sensitive genealogical information and personal details. With a vast database of family histories and DNA data, ensuring the security of your account protects against unauthorized access, identity theft, and privacy breaches. Ancestry.com's commitment to privacy necessitates users' active involvement in adopting security measures to maintain the integrity of their family history data.*

Question: What resources are available to help me understand and implement data security best practices on Ancestry.com?

Answer: *Ancestry.com provides comprehensive resources to help you understand and implement data security best practices.*

Visit their Privacy Statement and Security of Personal Information pages for in-depth insights into how your data is handled and protected.

Additionally, explore Ancestry.com's Privacy Philosophy for a clear understanding of their commitment to safeguarding your information.

Familiarize yourself with these resources to enhance your knowledge and ensure a secure experience on the platform.

Question: What are Ancestry.com's privacy policies, and why are they important?

Answer*: Ancestry.com's privacy policies, outlined in their Privacy Statement, are crucial for protecting your personal information. These policies detail how your data is* *collected, stored, and processed, emphasizing responsible handling and security measures.*

Understanding these policies empowers you to make informed decisions about sharing your family history information. Ancestry.com prioritizes being a responsible steward of your data, and adherence to their privacy policies ensures a trustworthy and secure environment for your genealogical pursuits.

Question: How does Ancestry.com handle the personal information I provide?

Answer: *Ancestry.com is committed to being a responsible steward of your personal information. They employ various security measures, such as encryption, to prevent fraud and protect sensitive details like payment information.*

Your privacy is a top priority, and Ancestry.com has a longstanding history of safeguarding personal information for over two decades.

Your data is handled responsibly, and you can trust Ancestry.com to provide a secure platform for building and preserving your family history.

Question: Can I control who can access my family history information on Ancestry.com?

Answer: *Yes, you have control over who accesses your family history on Ancestry.com. The platform provides privacy settings that allow you to determine the visibility of your family tree. You can choose between public, private, or unindexed privacy settings. By opting for a private or unindexed tree, you restrict access to only those you invite or make your tree available for search without revealing living people's details.*

Question: What information is considered public on Ancestry.com?

Answer: *In public family trees on Ancestry.com, most information is viewable and searchable, excluding details about living individuals. This includes facts, photos, and sources from deceased relatives. Ancestry.com prioritizes privacy and ensures living individuals' information remains confidential* *while still allowing you to share and collaborate on ancestral information.*

Question: How can I make my family history information more private on Ancestry.com?

Answer: *To enhance privacy on Ancestry.com, consider changing your tree's settings to private or unindexed. Navigate to "Trees," select your family tree, and then choose "Tree Settings." Opting for a private or unindexed tree limits access, ensuring your family history details are shared only with those you invite or, in the case of unindexed, making it available for search without revealing living individuals' information.*

Question: Will my uploaded photos and documents be visible to the public on Ancestry.com?

Answer: *Uploaded photos and documents are subject to the privacy settings of your family tree. In public trees, these items are viewable and searchable by others. To restrict access, set your family tree to private or unindexed,* *ensuring that your uploaded photos and documents remain private or semi-private.*

Question: Can I control who can edit and contribute to my family history information?

Answer: Absolutely! Ancestry.com allows you to manage contributors to your family tree. You can invite family members to collaborate, control their level of access, and limit editing permissions. This ensures that your family history information remains accurate and collaborative while under your control.

Question: How does Ancestry.com protect my data from unauthorized access?

Answer: *Ancestry.com employs robust security measures, including encryption and fraud prevention methods, to safeguard your personal information. These measures are designed to prevent unauthorized access and ensure the confidentiality of your data.*

Question: Does Ancestry.com share my data with third parties?

Answer: *Ancestry.com is committed to being a responsible steward of your data and does not sell your personal information to third parties. Your data's privacy is a top priority, and Ancestry.com follows stringent measures to protect it.*

Question: How does Ancestry.com use cookies and tracking technologies?

Answer: *Ancestry.com utilizes cookies and tracking technologies to enhance your user experience. These technologies help personalize content, analyze site usage, and improve overall functionality. You can manage your cookie preferences in your browser settings.*

Question: Can I opt out of receiving emails and notifications from Ancestry.com?

Answer: *Yes, you can customize your email preferences on Ancestry.com. Navigate to your account settings and adjust notification* *preferences to tailor your experience according to your preferences.*

Question: How can I request access to or correction of my personal information on Ancestry.com?

Answer: *Ancestry.com provides avenues for requesting access to or correction of your personal information. Refer to their support or contact page to find the appropriate channels for making such requests.*

Question: What should I do if I have concerns or questions about Ancestry.com's privacy policies?

Answer: *If you have concerns or questions about Ancestry.com's privacy policies, the best course of action is to review their detailed privacy statements available on their official website. Additionally, you can reach out to Ancestry.com's customer support for clarification and assistance with any privacy-related queries.*

Additional Resources:

1. *Creating an Ancestry® Password*
2. *Genealogy Shorts – Ancestry enables Two-Factor Authentication*
3. *Security of Personal Information - Ancestry*
4. *Ancestry® Privacy Statement*
5. *Security of Personal Information*
6. *Your privacy is important to you. That's why it's so ...*
7. *Privacy for Your Family Tree - Ancestry*
8. *Family Tree Privacy - Ancestry® Support*
9. *Your privacy is important to you. That's why it's so ...*
10. *Family Tree Privacy*
11. *Privacy for Your Family Tree - Ancestry*

Other Books Available on Amazon
Liahona Publications

Sudoku Puzzles

Sudoku Bliss for All Ages:
Dive into the world of Sudoku
with our puzzle book

Notary Public Logbook

** 8.5 x 11 & 6 x 9 Paperback **

Our Notary Public Logbook is your key
to efficient and precise
record-keeping.

The Magic of Enchanted Adventures

*** E-Book & PaperBack***

A series that takes readers on a
journey through a magical world
filled with wonder, excitement

FamilySearch FAQ

** E-Book & PaperBack **

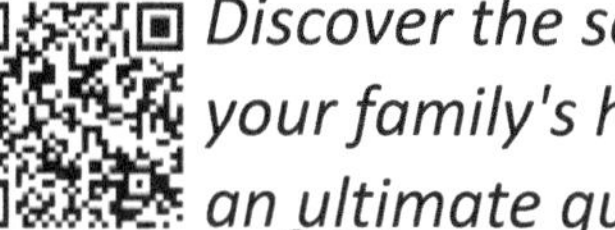

Discover the secrets to unveiling
your family's history with
an ultimate guide to genealogy.

www.ingramcontent.com/pod-product-compliance
Ingram Content Group UK Ltd.
Pitfield, Milton Keynes, MK11 3LW, UK
UKHW041857190726
13854UKWH00002B/944